PRAISE FOR **FOB DOC**

"Captain Ray Wiss left an extremely successful medical practice to
volunteer as a medical officer with the Canadian Forces in Afghanistan.
FOB *Doc* gives a clear picture from the coal face of why we are there and
what our soldiers have accomplished. This book pares away the rheto-
ric to present the soldier and his work with pride and professionalism."

BRIGADIER GENERAL PETER ATKINSON
Director General—Operations, Canadian Forces Strategic Joint Staff

"Ray's experience as a soldier and an emergency physician gives him
a unique clarity of vision which he trains on everything he sees on the
front lines in Afghanistan, from moral and medical aspects to social
and strategic issues. He is a natural teacher. After reading his diary,
you will understand Canada's mission in a whole new light."

HOWARD OVENS
Director, Schwartz/Reisman Emergency Centre, Mount Sinai Hospital, Toronto

"Dr. Ray Wiss has a hyperactive practice in clinical medicine and particularly in teaching emergency ultrasound all across Canada. He wrote FOB Doc to convince his friends that, in going to work in a combat zone for soldier's wages, he hadn't gone off the deep end. He has succeeded. After reading this book, you will have a much clearer understanding of why we are fighting in Afghanistan and of what is at stake."

DR. MICHEL GARNER
Chief, Emergency Department, Hôpital du Sacré-Cœur, Montréal

"FOB Doc was born from Ray's daily journal entries about his Afghan medical mission. His diary's main purpose was to provide an educational record for his daughter. As you read FOB Doc, you will witness how Ray provided care with humour and distinction to soldiers and civilians alike. You will also gain a new understanding of Canada's required role in Afghanistan. Ray's front line accounts are a witness to his success as a father, physician and friend."

SCOTT WILSON
Clinical Chief, Emergency Services, Eastern Health, St. John's, NL

A WAR DIARY

A Doctor on the Front Lines in Afghanistan

FOB DOC

Captain Ray Wiss, M.D.

Foreword by **General Rick Hillier**

DOUGLAS & McINTYRE

D&M PUBLISHERS INC.

Vancouver/Toronto/Berkeley

Douglas & McIntyre
A division of D&M Publishers Inc.
2323 Quebec Street, Suite 201
Vancouver, BC Canada V5T 4S7
www.dmpibooks.com

Library and Archives Canada Cataloguing in Publication
Wiss, Ray, 1959–
FOB doc : a doctor on the front lines in Afghanistan : a war diary / Ray Wiss.

ISBN 978-1-55365-472-8

1. Wiss, Ray, 1959–. 2. Afghan War, 2001– —Personal narratives, Canadian.
3. Canada—Armed Forces—Afghanistan—Medical personnel—Biography.
4. Afghan War, 2001– —Participation, Canadian. 5. Physicians—Afghanistan—Biography.
6. Physicians—Canada—Biography. I. Title.
DS371.413.W58 2009   958.104′7092   C2009-903758-0

Editing by John Eerkes-Medrano
Jacket design by Peter Cocking
Jacket photographs courtesy of Ray Wiss
Text design by Naomi MacDougall

All illustrations courtesy of the author, except for p. 30 (top and bottom) and pp. 197 to 207, courtesy Combat Camera Team, Department of National Defence (DND), reproduced with the permission of the Minister of Public Works and Government Services, 2009; p. 55 (two maps), courtesy Eric Leinberger; p. 192, artwork by and courtesy of Silvia Pecota; p. 208 (top), courtesy MCpl Ken Fenner, Combat Camera, and (bottom), artwork by and courtesy of Silvia Pecota.

Printed and bound in Canada by Friesens
Printed on acid-free paper that is forest friendly (100% post-consumer recycled paper) and has been processed chlorine free or printed on paper that comes from sustainable forests managed under the Forest Stewardship Council
Distributed in the U.S. by Publishers Group West.

We gratefully acknowledge the financial support of the Canada Council for the Arts, the British Columbia Arts Council, the Province of British Columbia through the Book Publishing Tax Credit, and the Government of Canada through the Book Publishing Industry Development Program (BPIDP) for our publishing activities.

For my daughter, Michelle

Why do soldiers risk their present, if not for their future?

"If you are neutral in situations of injustice, you have chosen the side of the oppressor. If an elephant has its foot on the tail of a mouse and you say that you are neutral, the mouse will not appreciate your neutrality."

ARCHBISHOP DESMOND TUTU

CONTENTS

Foreword

IF I HAVE HEARD CANADIAN SOLDIERS say, once, that they wish every Canadian, from coast to coast to coast, could spend one or two days in some of the hellholes these servicemen and women temporarily call home, then I've heard them say it a million times. They say it to express their frustration with the superficial concerns that Canadians are perceived to have for the rest of the world—that is, we must do everything possible to help, but not if it gets really hard or expensive or interferes with our lives—as well as their difficulty in articulating the difference between Canada and the rest of the world. These men and women who serve our country in our nation's uniform want all Canadians—young and old, both those born here and those recently arrived—to appreciate what a great country we have, what an affluent life we live and why we have a responsibility towards those who desperately need our help, whether we find it hard or not.

Obviously all Canadians can't visit or live in places like Afghanistan, but they can do it figuratively by reading FOB *Doc*. In this book, in a very real and emotional way, Ray Wiss fills the gap in our education concerning much that goes on outside our borders. FOB *Doc* leaves one feeling proud to be Canadian, emotional when reading about our sons and daughters who have been wounded or killed, and clear about the evils that lurk in our world—evils that sometimes need to be confronted, no matter the cost.

Ray's description of his tour in Kandahar and of the variety of his experiences—from the trip to Afghanistan to the instant and overwhelming impact of sand and heat, his work at the Role 3 Hospital, the vagaries of operational transport, insects and bugs, accommodation, and eating and socializing facilities—is so realistic that it puts us there, with Canadians that we know and with their friends from around the world. We are there during the boring times, in those minutes of sheer terror, at Christmas and while Ray's comrades talk to their families back in Canada. If a picture is worth a thousand words, Ray has shown us that picture and has used the words to create an experience we all can share.

Central to this book, though, is something that is fortunately unfamiliar to the vast majority of Canadians—war and all its implications. Like Ray Wiss, surrounded by the images and stories of the men and women with him, we get to see, through his eyes, the toughness and professionalism of those Canadian soldiers, tempered by their absolute humanity and kindness. We feel, with him and with them, their pride in being Canadian, in representing in this far-flung corner of the world a country that Afghans can only fantasize about living in. We get to understand the equipment they have and use so well—not in the terms that come across on Discovery Channel, but in a way that lets us say, "Yeah, I got it." We learn what an ARV is, and we connect with the young Canadians who operate the vehicle. We also get to feel the basic, rugged accommodations, the "bagged" meals that, although tasty, get monotonous after days of nothing else.

We come to see that human side of soldiering, when being killed or killing is something you deal with day after day. Ray unveils for us the historical truths of men and women in combat and of how they respond: with incredible skills, honed as never before in history and enabled by cutting-edge technology, and with compassion that avoids hurting the innocent Afghan victims caught in a war zone, even if that compassion means letting Taliban fighters escape—knowing that they will return to attack you again.

Ray puts us in the middle of the gallows humour that develops in these environments. Instantly, we go from that humour to grief, farewells, coping and remembrance with our national treasures in uniform when they lose their lives, whether because of direct fire, faceless roadside bombs or heart-wrenching battlefield accidents. The scenes at the unit medical station in FOB Lynx or FOB Leopard, or at Kandahar Air Field during a ramp ceremony, are all too real and unforgettable. In short, Ray puts context around what many Canadians *do* see about Afghanistan—the return of Canadian soldiers in coffins.

FOB *Doc*, however, is not only about the daily life, the grind, dedication and sacrifice of Canadians and their allies and friends. It also is a picture of the very soul of Afghans, those most persecuted of people living in one of the harshest places on earth, unfortunate enough to exist at a crossroads used by invaders since time immemorial. Whether it deals with the Afghan National Army soldier's stoicism after being wounded, the humour that comes from encountering those "different" individuals that always seem to be present in a crowd, the brutal regime that was the Taliban or the pitiful existence of children caught up in violence—often without family support structures and, most sadly, without hope—this book's descriptions and photos of ordinary Afghans are compelling. Rare is the Canadian who will not be moved by their terrible circumstances and their challenges in life. Even rarer is the Canadian who won't compare his or her own life of ease and, yes, luxury, with that of the boy who has a burned body and who will be handicapped for life, when relatively minor surgery could have lessened the impact. This, in a country where one's physical abilities often mean the difference between life and death!

It was easy for me, after much time in Afghanistan, to relate to the stories and descriptions in this book and to believe that Canadians would find it enthralling. So I used as a test case the reaction of my wife, who picked up the book without knowing what it was, started reading it and could not stop. She thought the book was amazing. Ray, she believed, had put a face on a country, people, mission and sacrifice in a way that brought them to life, putting into context much of what she had heard or seen elsewhere.

Ray poses two questions as he returns to Canada, to his family and their happy and complete life. Two questions that all Canadians should consider and answer. First: are the Afghan civilians—those men, women and children, hardworking, dignified and dirt poor but still with a sense of humour, hope and determination that puts others to shame—worth protecting? Canada's government, on behalf of all Canadians, has determined that they are. Canada's soldiers, those who bear the brunt of that determination, believe that also, and their actions—not words but actions—articulate Canada's belief. Most Canadians agree and support those actions.

The second question is a little more troubling for many Canadians. Are the Taliban so bad, so evil, that they must be confronted with lethal force? For Ray, the answer is an emphatic "Yes." Somehow, Canadians in many parts of our sheltered society, in our well-maintained cities, snuggled inside our "cradle to grave" social care system, often too uninterested to exercise basic rights such as voting for their representatives in an election, seem to think that violent, murderous men (and the occasional woman) can be influenced, neutralized, removed or persuaded to adopt peaceful approaches through diplomatic, financial or developmental pressures. Ray strongly disagrees with this premise. He closes his diary by asking readers who are unsure about the mission or who oppose it to inform themselves as well as possible. Overwhelming proof of the immorality of the Taliban, through evidence of evil, violent actions, and of the need to confront them militarily, is there for all to see. Unfortunately, for most Canadians, all they know of the mission comes from the media focus on our casualties.

Doc Wiss has lived it. And through his eyes, in his words, shaped by his evident common sense and supported by his pictures, all Canadians can live it too. Canadians can better appreciate their country, which tops the UN charts, after "visiting" Afghanistan, a country on the bottom of the charts, through *FOB Doc*. I encourage you to read this book, to think about what it is to be Canadian in the context of this story and to encourage your family and friends to read it. And I encourage all of you to give thanks for men and women like Ray Wiss and the comrades he describes.

xv

GENERAL RICK HILLIER | March 2009

Preface

AM AN EMERGENCY MEDICINE (EM) specialist. It is axiomatic in my field that the story we get may not always be completely accurate. Patients will often try to diminish their personal involvement in the events leading to their injury. A common variant of this, instantly recognizable by any EM physician, begins with the words:

"I was just standing there, minding my own business, when some dude…"

This is usually followed by a nose-stretching account of how the patient has no idea why the "dude" in question shot/stabbed/hit him in the head with a brick, etc....

This diary started much the same way. I was in Afghanistan, just standing there, minding my own business, when some dude (actually, it was a "dudette") suggested I write something to explain what I was doing there. I wrote that first letter to help my friends understand what had motivated me. The same person suggested I keep a diary for my daughter to read when she was older.

So I started jotting things down. I sent a first batch of entries to my friends about a month later, along with a letter explaining the goals of the diary. I kept sending entries until I returned home.

The exercise was quite beneficial: it kept me busy, and it allowed me to share what I was going through with family and friends. I thought it would end there.

I was still in Afghanistan, still minding my own business, when my hometown newspaper asked that portions of my diary be released for publication. As a serving officer, I sought the approval of the Canadian Forces. This led to the diary being read by various officers in the Health Services, Public Affairs and Operational Security branches.

I was surprised by the reaction of those first readers who were not related to me through blood or friendship. All of them thought the diary was worthy of a greater readership, and they encouraged me to get the work published.

I was pleased by the compliments, but this presented me with a bit of a challenge. I had been published before, but only in emergency medicine circles. After I got to be fairly well known in my field, people would spontaneously ask me to write articles on various subjects. I would then bang something out and hand it in. Some time after that, by a process into which I had little insight, my words would come out in print. Published I may have been, but I had little idea of how to go about getting my diary into print in the non-medical world.

Google to the rescue! Search "Canadian Publisher" and see what pops up. Right under the first heading is a subheading titled "How to get published." I did pretty much exactly what they suggested. This is not to say that the process was effortless: I was rejected repeatedly—a novel experience for a doctor. But persistence paid off, and the good folks at D&M Publishers Inc. decided to take a chance on the project, a decision no doubt influenced by the fact that I brought my utterly charming three-year-old daughter to the key negotiating session with Scott McIntyre (the "M" in D&M).

Success in getting the contract signed, however, presented me with a moral dilemma. I had never intended to sell the diary for personal gain, and it sat very badly with me to do so when some of the brothers-in-arms I had written about would not be coming back. As a soldier, I wanted it to be clear that I had gone to Afghanistan to support the mission, not to write a book.

The solution to this problem was easy: give any profits I might make to the Military Families Fund (MFF). The MFF, created by General Rick Hillier in 2007, is a very nimble organization that can, with a minimum of red tape and with remarkable speed, respond to the needs of Canadian Forces members whose lives have been affected by the disruptions that are an inevitable part of military life. The Canadian Forces takes very good care of its people, to be sure: the MFF is there for the "nice to have" as well as the "need to have right now" items. It provides a way for Canadians to materially express their support for the troops.

I rejoined the army and went to Afghanistan to support the members of the Canadian Forces. By purchasing this diary, you have joined me in continuing to do so long after my return.

Thank you for that.

A Note on the People, Places and Pictures

THE PEOPLE As I mention above, I did not set out to write a book. I was writing very personal letters to close friends, so I mostly described my own actions and feelings. Had I known where this project would eventually end up, I would have spent far more time describing the people I was with. There were a great many Canadian soldiers I met in Afghanistan whose actions richly deserve to be recorded and remembered but whose stories do not appear in these pages. I regret having missed the opportunity to write about them.

THE PLACES AND PICTURES Our country is at war. As a serving officer in the Canadian Forces, my priority is to ensure that nothing I do harms our combat efficiency. I therefore worked closely with the Operational Security (OpSec) branch to ensure that this book gave nothing away that our enemies might use to any advantage, no matter how small. This process had no impact on the story. The OpSec personnel often merely asked that a sentence be rewritten to make a detail somewhat vaguer, rather than removing the sentence completely. You would have to follow my original text line by line, comparing it with the final text, to be able to detect the passages that were changed. Not a single paragraph's meaning or import was altered.

The same cannot be said for place names and pictures. Some places have been given fictitious names, and some pictures have had militarily sensitive elements cropped out. Again, these changes are so subtle that they have no impact on the story.

Veterans of the Afghanistan war will immediately recognize what has been modified or removed. They will also know to keep that to themselves.

Introduction

CANADA HAS BEEN AT WAR in Afghanistan since 2001. One might think that, by now, most Canadians would be quite conversant with the history of the region, the key historical facts and the underlying premises of the main issues. Unfortunately, this is not the case.

The war in Afghanistan divides our country pretty much right down the middle. But this division is much more emotional than factual. I have been surprised, both before and after my tour of duty in Afghanistan, at the lack of hard knowledge on both sides of the debate. For every person who viscerally opposes the war because "war is bad," you can find someone who enthusiastically supports it because "those Muslims are out to get us." Neither of these views is particularly helpful when our country is having the most serious debate it can: deciding to send its sons and daughters into harm's way.

I therefore began writing this diary to explain to approximately one hundred friends why I had chosen to interrupt a very successful medical career to serve my country at war. I thought the best way to do this would be to write about all aspects of my life, and the life of my fellow soldiers. Each daily (or so) entry would focus on a particular subject or event and examine it in detail.

As I was sending this back to Canada electronically, I had to be circumspect about certain details of our operations. You never know who might be listening, and it can be a fatal mistake to underestimate an enemy you believe to be less technologically sophisticated than you are. Within those confines, I hoped to paint an accurate picture of our mission.

I began writing when I got to Kandahar. The first entry I wrote there, as you will see, reads like a travelogue with guns. But as I was finishing that first entry, I was confronted with the reality of war: two Canadians were killed in action. Before I could adjust to the time change, I was standing on the tarmac at the Kandahar Air Field saying a solemn goodbye to our fallen. This prompted me to write a completely different letter, one that was much more political and that sought to explain my beliefs and my motivations for choosing this course of action.

As was the case for my friends in 2007, I will introduce the diary with that first letter. When you have finished reading it, you may not agree with my beliefs. But you certainly will know where I stand.

Why Am I Here?

Dear Friends,

Although this is the first letter you will receive from me, it is not the first letter I have written here in Kandahar. I had nearly finished that letter a few days ago. It was, as you might have expected, quite whimsical and focused on the lighter aspects of the trip over and of actually being here. Hard though it may be to believe, there were quite a few humorous moments, mostly centred on the rigours of living on the base.

I was about to send that first letter when our most recent casualties occurred. Now, it is too much at odds with the way I am feeling for me to complete it. I have been to a ramp ceremony and have seen our fallen go by. That is a watershed event, both in my life and in my participation in this war. So I will write another, more serious letter instead. The lighter one will have to wait.

I suppose I should start by explaining what I am doing here.

First, some historical context. Before World War Two, soldiers went beyond their national borders almost exclusively for narrow economic interests. Military expeditions either sought to establish empires, by the conquest of technologically inferior areas, or to defend empires against similarly armed opponents.

World War Two saw the first instances of soldiers going "overseas" to fight for reasons which were fundamentally moral. The Nazis and the Japanese militarists were pure evil—their destruction was a moral imperative. Their crimes were so great that they forced the world to develop the concept of "crimes against humanity"—behaviour so barbarous that it offended the very nature of human beings.

In the last two decades, we have seen the emergence of "muscular" peacekeeping missions. Robust military action has been used to defend civilians with little, if any, secondary gain for the nations sending troops. The Australian mission in East Timor and Canada's mission in Bosnia are archetypal examples of this. We then saw the first example of a war whose explicit goal was the defence of civilians: the NATO attack on Serbia to counter the Serbs' actions in Kosovo.

As much as these examples are remarkably positive, they remain the exception. In the last decade, the world stood by while genocidal actions took place in Rwanda and (arguably) in Sierra Leone and Liberia. And we are doing little more than wringing our hands while the Janjaweed militia tries its hand at extermination in Darfur.*

This brings us to Afghanistan today. I think a lot of Canadians have trouble distinguishing this war from the one in Iraq. The Iraqi situation is one a lot of us, myself included, have difficulty with. But Afghanistan

---

* The Janjaweed are an Arab militia who are trying to wrest control of the Darfur province of Sudan from its mainly African inhabitants. They are more or less openly supported by the Sudanese government, which denies this while simultaneously allowing its armed forces to participate in attacks on civilians targeted by the Janjaweed. Precise numbers are notoriously difficult to ascertain, but it seems certain that more than a quarter-million people have been murdered by the Janjaweed and their Sudanese allies.

is completely different. We are here at the request of the United Nations who, through Resolution 1833, asked for assistance with security in this country. We remain at the request of the duly elected government of Afghanistan. Finally, Canada has nothing to gain materially from helping one of the poorest countries in the world. Afghanistan is not Iraq!*

Whatever is going on in Iraq does not change the fact that the Taliban are among the worst abusers to walk the face of the earth. Their reign here from 1996 to 2001 was one of unmitigated terror. Anyone doubting their savagery has only to compare the way the two sides in this war fight.

Coalition forces use their heavy weapons in a very limited and judicious manner. Firing them from beyond close range must be authorized by the area commander. These weapons cause more peripheral damage and have a higher risk of causing civilian casualties. We will often let an enemy get away rather than taking the chance of harming the innocent.

The Taliban, on the other hand, routinely plant bombs where it is certain that civilian deaths will occur. This fall, they attacked a small group of Afghan policemen who were shopping at the local market near one of our forward operating bases (FOBs). They managed to injure a few of their targets, but thirty-six civilians were killed or maimed. This is a routine occurrence here—many of the Taliban roadside bombs do little more than dent our armoured vehicles, but they often kill or injure bystanders, particularly children.

Since it has been in the news a lot recently, let us also examine how both sides treat prisoners. Regardless of how one feels about the legality of Omar Khadr's internment, he (like all Guantanamo detainees) is getting food and medical care on a par with most Canadians. While I believe he should be punished for his actions, I am quite proud that my country is having a real debate about his fate. I support his right to a fair

---

* *Postscript, April 28, 2008:* The common inability to differentiate between the two wars takes on proportions that would be farcical if they were not so tragic. An officer who served at one of the FOBs that I was assigned to was asked why we were still in Afghanistan, since "we already caught Saddam Hussein." This degree of ignorance is deeply hurtful to veterans.

trial. If he is returned to Canada, I expect our country to fully respect his rights. The Americans do much the same thing. When things go off the rails, as they did at Haditha and Abu Ghraib, they eventually send their people to jail.

In comparison, we recently found the bodies of five Afghan National Army soldiers the Taliban had captured. Before they were killed, these soldiers were tortured with a brutality that is difficult to conceive and that would take a couple of paragraphs to describe. The perpetrators of this atrocity will be celebrated in their own ranks.

For those who have difficulty with the fact that we are allied with the Americans in this war, I would remind them that in World War Two our ally against the Nazis was Joseph Stalin. It is fairly easy to make the case that Stalin, over the long term, was an even worse mass murderer than Adolf Hitler. It was nonetheless appropriate to ally ourselves with the Russian dictator. The Americans are not perfect, but by no stretch of the imagination are they like Stalin. As a nation and a people they are committed to democracy; they are well intentioned and fundamentally honourable.

Given my druthers, I would rather be participating in a combat mission aimed at destroying the Janjaweed. What is going on in Darfur is even worse than what was happening in Afghanistan. The geopolitical reality for our country is that we cannot act in Darfur, but we *can* act here. That "geopolitical space" is created by the Americans.

Churchill said that "the only thing harder than fighting a war with allies . . . is fighting one without them." Since this is a moral war, I am happy to have the Americans by our side. We can agree to disagree about other issues while we get the job done here.

Bottom line: I completely support our mission in Afghanistan, and I want to do my part. I believe our country is engaged in a just cause and our soldiers need help. That is a call I have to answer. The world isn't "the way it is"; it is the way we make it.

Sounds hopelessly idealistic, perhaps, but that's how I want to live my life.

Regards, *Ray*

A Glossary

Military-speak

The people reading this diary were a very mixed bag. A lot of them were medical, some of them were military, some of them were both and some of them were neither. It was a challenge to write about military medicine to such a diverse audience. The medical stuff I could write about in layman's terms, but there was no way to tell this story without a fair bit of military-speak. For the majority of my friends who, like the readers of this book, are non-military, I started this diary with a brief glossary.

ANA **(Afghan National Army)** The most respected branch of the Afghan government. It is developing into an effective fighting force with minimal corruption. Within a few years, it should be able to defeat the Taliban in most encounters, with some help from Coalition forces (mostly in the form of air support).

ANP **(Afghan National Police)** A disaster. Virtually untrained, completely corrupt. ANP officers get sent out in small groups to tiny outposts, where they smoke dope and rob the local population because they (the police) are often not paid—their commanders keep the money for themselves. When attacked by the Taliban, they either run away or are massacred. *So why not just fire them all and be done with it?* Because one of the key elements of a functioning society is a respected and effective police force. Like it or not, we have to make this part of the puzzle work if we are to stabilize Afghanistan.

Addendum, May 25, 2009: I wrote that entry in late 2007. As I prepare to return in mid-2009, I have been e-mailing my colleagues in the combat area. Apparently, a significant number of ANP units are engaging in paramilitary operations entirely on their own, having "graduated" to the point where they no longer need mentors or accompanying Coalition troops. Something must be working.

ARTILLERY (a.k.a. cannons) Heavy guns that fire massive shells tens of kilometres. Our standard artillery piece is the M777 155 mm gun. This means that the diameter of the shell that leaves the cannon is 155 mm.

ARV (pronounced "arv"; armoured recovery vehicle) A tracked vehicle, built on the chassis of a Leopard tank, that functions as a mobile repair shop for the tanks.

CF (Canadian Forces) The Canadian army, navy and air force. Used to be the Canadian *Armed* Forces, but that was felt to be too aggressive and not nice enough to be truly Canadian. This, of course, is complete bullshit. To paraphrase General Rick Hillier: We are not like any other government department. We are the Canadian Forces. We kill people.

COALITION The term used to describe the forty-two nations involved in the fight against the Taliban. Although this is a UN-sanctioned NATO mission, many countries that are not NATO members are part of the Coalition (France being probably the most notable example).

FOB (pronounced "fob"; forward operating base) An area where Canadian soldiers are based, in territory where Taliban activity is high, near a population concentration. A permanent installation from which vehicle-borne and foot-borne patrols can operate. We sleep in bunkers, eat ration packs and hand-wash clothing. Life is austere.

FRAG VEST (fragmentation vest, a.k.a. flak jacket or body armour) A vest that covers the entire torso with Kevlar (which can stop shrapnel) and has a metal plate over the heart and lungs front and back (which can stop bullets).

GDMO (general duty medical officer) A doctor in the CF who is not a specialist; more accurately, a doctor who is not recognized by the CF to be a specialist. A few doctors working in the CF, myself included, are emergency medicine specialists. The CF, however, does not need full-time emergency physicians: none of our bases have hospitals or free-standing emergency departments. EM specialists who work for the CF are therefore classed as GDMOS.

IED (improvised explosive device, a.k.a. roadside bomb) A big pile of explosives, usually harvested from unexploded bombs or artillery shells and stuffed into a big cooking pot, which the Taliban bury in the road and detonate when we get close. IEDS cause most of the casualties Canada suffers in Afghanistan. They can be detonated by pressure plates (someone steps on or drives over the device), direct control (by wire) or remote control (by radio or cell phone). There are also SIEDS (suicide IEDS—guys with the explosive vests under their jackets), VBIEDS (vehicle-borne IEDS—cars packed with explosives and remote detonated when a patrol goes by) and SVBIEDS (suicide vehicle–borne IEDS—cars packed with explosives that the attackers try to drive into one of our convoys before blowing themselves up). BBIED (bicycle-borne IED) and DBIED (donkey-borne IED) are self-explanatory.

While you may have heard about IEDS, it is important to realize that you have only read about the ones that kill or hurt our soldiers. You don't hear about the large number we detect and destroy, both with our excellent high-tech mine-clearing equipment and with brave soldiers probing the ground with their bayonets, like their forefathers did. You don't hear about the large number of IEDs that detonate, but do no more than scratch the paint on our armoured vehicles. You don't hear about the ones neutralized by our effective electronic counter-measures. And you don't hear about the times we find the trigger-man, sitting in the desert with his wire or his cell phone, and kill him before he has the chance to fire his weapon.

KAF (pronounced "kaf"; Kandahar Air Field) The main Coalition base in the south of Afghanistan—the area where the Taliban have the most support. Home to about twelve thousand people, including around a thousand civilians from all over the world who are here on contract to service the various forces. Living conditions are quite good. You get a bed with a mattress, a hot shower every day, easy Internet access and good food. There is even a Tim Hortons! Built too close to the local sewage treatment plant, though, so when the wind blows in the wrong direction, you want to barf.

The danger at KAF comes from Taliban rockets, which are launched from beyond the perimeter defences of the base. These perimeter defences, which have never been breached, are colloquially called "the wire"—a reference to the barbed wire that is used for much of those defences. At any one time, there are approximately 2,800 Canadians in Afghanistan, but only a third of them are combat troops who go "outside the wire." The remainder stay at KAF for their entire tour.

KANDAHAR The province in southern Afghanistan where Canadians have been fighting since late 2005. Not to be confused with KAF (see above). This is the home turf of the Taliban and the area where they have the most support, making it the most difficult military assignment in the country. It's an area studiously avoided by many of our NATO allies, who forbid their forces to be deployed here. Conspiracy theories abound as to why Canadians are fighting in Kandahar province, such as: Jean Chrétien wanted to make amends to George W. Bush for not joining him in Iraq, or General Rick Hillier fooled everyone and got us involved in an "unexpected war" (to quote a popular book). There is a far simpler, and much more credible, explanation. In 2005, with America's attention diverted to Iraq, it was evident that the Taliban— after recuperating in their tribal areas in Pakistan—were going to be resurgent in Kandahar. Somebody had to go there and take them on. The best troops available to NATO, the Canadians, were asked to execute this mission, and they accepted. That's what soldiers do. Anyone paying attention to what the Canadian Forces was saying at that time will recall that our leaders were explicitly clear: the move to Kandahar would bring greater casualties. There was nothing "unexpected" about it.

You don't win wars by playing it safe. You have to go after the enemy, preferably in *his* backyard. If you don't, you will eventually find yourself fighting in your own.

LAV **(pronounced "lav"; light armoured vehicle)** The main fighting vehicle of the Canadian Forces. Armed with a 25 mm cannon and a co-axial 7.62 mm machine gun (that is, it fires in exactly the same direction as the cannon). It also has a 7.62 mm machine gun that the crew commander can operate. The only Canadian woman killed in Afghanistan was Captain Nichola Goddard, who died in May 2006, when she was hit in the head by shrapnel while standing in the hatch of her LAV directing fire.

LEOPARD TANK This seventy-ton monster is almost impervious to IEDs, and its cannon can outreach everything the enemy has. Leopards are used to support infantry operations and for mine clearing. Some are equipped with rollers, which are attached to the front of the tank and are designed to detonate mines before the tank rolls onto them. Others are equipped with plows, which serve the same purpose.

MMU **(Multinational Medical Unit)** The main hospital at KAF. Also called "the Role 3 Hospital," which means it has the capacity to do surgery. Commanded by a Canadian and dominated by Canadian staff, mostly military but with the occasional civilian thrown in.

MORTAR Same general idea as artillery—a tube that fires a smaller bomb over a few kilometres. Our standard mortars are 60 mm and 81 mm.

NIGHT VISION In earlier wars, it was often the less technologically sophisticated side that preferred to operate at night. The more technologically advanced side was always vastly superior in two areas: heavy weapons and aircraft. Decreased visibility reduced the advantages provided by these weapons. The Viet Cong in Vietnam and the mujahedeen who fought the Russians here in the 1980s, for instance, made excellent use of the cover of darkness.

Since around 1990, night vision technology has become so reliable and cheap that Western armies are now able to issue these devices to every soldier in the field. This completely transforms the nighttime environment. Now the technologically advanced side rules the night.

OP (pronounced "op"; operation) A military manoeuvre of some kind. Not to be confused with...

OP (pronounced "oh-pee"; observation post) Exactly what the name implies, but it comes in many shapes and sizes. It can be a reinforced bunker full of troops or two soldiers with a radio hiding in a field.

PA (physician assistant) The most senior medic in the Canadian Forces, and able to do virtually everything an M.D. can do with regard to the first hour of trauma care. In Afghanistan, PAs run the medical teams deployed to the FOBs. Unfortunately for the CF, the civilian world is beginning to recognize these extremely well-trained health care professionals and is offering them jobs in civilian hospitals. As a result, the CF is having a harder and harder time covering the PA positions.

QRF (quick reaction force) A group of soldiers tasked to respond immediately to any crisis.

An ANA soldier with an RPG launcher

ROTO (rotation) The six- to seven-month period that a Canadian Battle Group is deployed to Kandahar. Sometimes used interchangeably with the term "tour," as in: "That guy is on his third tour in Afghanistan." The names and numbers of the different rotations are a source of much confusion, even in military circles, so a brief explanation is in order. I was in Kandahar during Roto 4, which deployed in the late summer of 2007. Canadians have been in Afghanistan for longer than the roto numbers imply. This is because we began numbering our rotos all over again when we moved from Kabul into Kandahar province in late 2005. At that time, the name of the operation also changed, from Operation Apollo (Kabul) to Operation Athena (Kandahar). Don't ask me why the CF has this thing for Greek mythology.

The CF also refers to the battle groups by the year they deployed and whether they were the first or the second to go that year. Roto 4 was also known as Task Force (or TF) 3-07. The battle group that deployed to Afghanistan in the spring of 2007 was known as Task Force 1-07. What happened to TF 2-07, you ask? Answer: the army always maintains two battle groups (or task forces) ready to go. One battle group deploys, while the other stays in Canada. In 2007, TF 01-07 and TF 03-07 deployed to Afghanistan, while TF 02-07 and TF 04-07 were kept at their home bases. The same was true in 2008 and 2009. While the level of readiness for the 02 and 04 task forces is lower than for those going to Afghanistan, they are nonetheless combat-ready and can be called upon to deal with anything unexpected at a moment's notice.

RPG (rocket-propelled grenade) A weapon that propels a small explosive charge out to a distance of about four hundred metres. In the photo, the bulbous green thing on the end is the grenade. The rest of the weapon is the launcher. After the grenade flies off, the tube can be reloaded with another round. The orange colouring on the soldier's nails is henna, which Afghan men commonly put on their fingernails.

TAC VEST (tactical vest) A vest that goes over the frag vest (see above) and has a bunch of pockets for canteens, ammunition, grenades, rations and so on. Fully loaded, these two vests weigh more than thirty back-strain-guaranteeing pounds!

UMS (unit medical station) The small and rudimentary, but quite effective, medical facility at a FOB.

The Diary

November 6, 2007 to March 3, 2008

NOVEMBER 6 | Departure

Going to war. What would you feel on that day? Fear? Determination? Excitement? For me, it wasn't like that. It wasn't like that at all.

First, I must explain that I am writing today's entry some eighteen months after the fact. I never intended for this diary to become a book, and I only started writing entries when I got to Kandahar. However, the logical starting point of any such diary has to be the day of departure, hence the late addition.

While some parts of that day are crystal clear, others are hazy. I do remember, very well, that when I left Sudbury to go to war in Afghanistan on November 6, 2007, I wasn't scared, determined or excited. What I did feel takes some explaining.

For me, going to war was a choice. A choice to leave family and friends and go towards discomfort and danger. When the process started, I had periods of self-doubt. No matter how much I believed in the mission, I couldn't help but question the wisdom of my decision. Most of the time, though, I was convinced I was doing the right thing. I had many long conversations in which I discussed Canada's mission, and my part in it, with several close friends and, above all, with my wife,

Claude. These conversations enabled me to better articulate what I felt: that this was a vital mission for Canada to be engaged in and that I had a role to play in it.

But as the departure date drew near, a shift occurred. It was subtle at first, but it became more pronounced as the days passed. I was engaged in frenetic preparations and started to worry that everything wouldn't get done in time, that my departure would be delayed. Having committed myself to go, I started to worry that I might not be able to leave as planned. But finally everything did get done, with about a week to spare.

You might think that I spent those last days reflecting on the enormity of what I was going to undertake. You might think I used the time to have several more long discussions with my wife. You might think that I became more aware of my own mortality. But I didn't.

During the final phase of the pre-deployment process, which lasted almost six weeks, I was so focused on the job at hand that I just wanted to *get going*. The waiting became almost excruciating. I wanted to be "over there" *now!* Since returning, I have learned that this is quite common—many veterans relate the same experience.

Not surprisingly, my relationship with my wife changed. We both began pulling back from each other, in subconscious anticipation of the upcoming separation. For Claude, it was also the preparation of a survival mechanism in case I did not return. A good friend of mine, a married man who had served in Afghanistan earlier, had warned me this would happen. But when it did, I was too far gone to be able to see it. I was already in Afghanistan in my mind.

So it was a quiet drive to the airport. Just Claude and me. I had said goodbye to my parents the day before and to our two-year-old daughter, Michelle, that morning. Claude had wondered whether it would be better to take Michelle with us to the airport but decided against it. She did not think that she would cry, but if she did she thought it better that Michelle did not see her doing so.

What did we say at the airport? We said we loved each other, of course, but mostly we took care of administrative details. "I'll be in Toronto for two days doing the last bits of paperwork and getting the last bits of gear. This is when I'll call. Then I fly out of Canada on

November 10. This is when I'll call. If I land when you're sleeping, I'll send a quick e-mail to let you know I am safely on the ground." To which Claude replied: "Safely on the ground . . . in a war zone. That will be one reassuring e-mail, all right!" Even at the worst of times, Claude manages to keep her ironic sense of humour.

We hugged one last time, but Claude could feel how much I wanted to get going. She let me go, waved at me through the window of the security area and walked away. She did not want to see my plane leave. No pictures were taken. For reasons I can't fully explain, I don't regret that.

I took my place on the plane and watched the northern Ontario landscape slip away. After all the preparation, I was on my way.

I was going to war.

Bizarrely, I started to relax.

NOVEMBER 10–14 | Getting to Kandahar the Hard Way

Call me Murphy. Whatever could have gone wrong with this trip did go wrong.

My departing flight from Canada was delayed for over twenty-four hours, so I only arrived at our staging base "somewhere in the Middle East" at 0200 on November 12, after a long and miserable flight with an interminable layover in Frankfurt. The flight was made more miserable by the significance of the destination, but not for the reasons you might expect. Normally, when crossing the pond, I take a sleeping pill to help me adjust to the time change. But sleeping pills can give you a bit of memory loss for several hours after you take them. On this trip I wanted to remember every detail, so I stayed awake most of the way. This may have been a bad move. I got to the Middle East exhausted and with my body still on Eastern Standard Time.

Given the hour, there was only a skeleton staff waiting to greet me and the other arriving soldiers. This was most unfortunate because, in a typical snafu caused by my delayed arrival, no one who was awake had any idea I was arriving. No one gets onto the base without proper documentation, part of which is the documentation that arrives *before* you

Last leg to Kandahar, reading *Lonely Planet Afghanistan* on a Herc

do, to advise the base of your upcoming stay. None of this was available to the people at the gate. The guards therefore inspected me, my luggage and my travel documents quite thoroughly before I was allowed in—not a lot of fun, when everyone else is already in bed.

The comedy of errors continued the next day. The people who had greeted me at the base at 0200 told me to report to the main office of the base at 0800 to figure out what was happening. When I showed up at the appointed hour the clerk said, "We missed you this morning." Apparently, I had been scheduled to fly out to Kandahar that very day at 0500. This earned me a "Where are you?" e-mail from my company commander.

Not much to say about this place. For security reasons, we call it "Camp Mirage" and try to pretend it does not exist. It is just a transit base for troops going to and from Afghanistan. For me, it was a forty-eight-hour blur of heat and jet lag. There is a strict "no pictures" rule on the base, which is a shame—there is a small, simple but quite moving monument here to our dead, which I would have wanted to record.

We mustered at 0500 on the 14th to place our gear on pallets (no carry-on!). Then we headed to the airfield to draw weapons and protective equipment. I was issued a pistol and a rifle as well as a helmet and a

The KAF Five-Star

flak jacket—which we call a frag vest, because it protects us from bomb *fragments*, a.k.a. shrapnel.

Speaking of the gear, it is exceptionally good. This is not to say that our army, while spending a lot of money on good equipment, does not do its best to be frugal. I have gear that, going by the names written on various pieces, has previously been issued to several other soldiers.

We then waited . . . and waited . . . and waited . . . for the aircraft to be ready. After two hours spent in the ever-increasing heat, we were loaded onto a C-130 Hercules for the trip to Kandahar Air Field (KAF), the main Coalition base in southern Afghanistan and home to the Canadian contingent there. After thirty minutes, we were unloaded as the Herc had some mechanical malfunction. After another hour on the now-stifling tarmac, we were loaded onto another Herc, which managed to get itself into the air.

The 2006 edition of *Lonely Planet Afghanistan* begins with the words: "By any stretch of the imagination, Afghanistan isn't the simplest country to travel in." Grammatically awkward, perhaps, but a useful tip!

Arrival in Kandahar is interesting. The "terminal building" is called TLS, for Taliban Last Stand. It still shows all the damage it suffered when the Coalition took it in 2001. It doesn't serve as a building per se, as

In the rocket shelter

the structure has never been restored. The name is so evocative that it has persisted through the years.

The heat and dust, even now in mid-November, hit me hard. Fortunately, the hospital had arranged for a vehicle to come by and collect me. It took me straight to my quarters to drop my gear off.

The "hard shacks" we live in have sheet metal walls and a concrete floor. I have a two-by-three-metre space (almost) in a room I share with three other health care types (a doc and two male nurses).

The bed is comfy and the temperature is well controlled, thanks to an air conditioner that sounds like a cement mixer. Good thing I brought superior earplugs—sleeping here will be a challenge.

The food here is excellent. We eat in a large "DFac" (army talk for "dining facility") run by a civilian contractor. It looks like any other large institutional cafeteria, so I am right at home. The only difference is that everyone who eats here is armed—you can't get in unless you are carrying a weapon.

The main risk at Kandahar Air Field (KAF) comes from rocket attacks. The Taliban were kind enough to organize one to celebrate my arrival. It hit as we were eating supper, and we had to go into shelters that are beside every building on the base. KAF, however, is gigantic. I heard the explosion, but it was so far away I had trouble telling exactly which direction the sound had come from. I noted that no one moved towards the shelters at more than a normal walk. Okay, maybe a tad faster than that.

I'm finally here. I have gone to war.*

---

* *Postscript, March 19, 2009:* That feeling of relaxation I felt when my plane left Sudbury? It was gone now.

First day at work...sort of. I am finding it surprisingly difficult to adjust to the time change. I wake up at 0100 every night and don't start to feel tired till 0600, so I went through the day in a bit of a daze. Be that as it may, here are the salient facts of working here.

The outfit I work for is officially called the Multinational Medical Unit, or MMU. This is a Canadian-led surgical hospital, which we also call a "Role 3 facility," the highest level of medical care the Canadian Forces deploys into a theatre of operations.

One part of the MMU is the trauma area, where the real action happens, with many trauma bays. Attached to this part are the inpatient beds and the ICU. The other part is a walk-in clinic affair that tends to the everyday needs of the KAF population. It can hold people overnight if they need minor stuff, like IV rehydration.

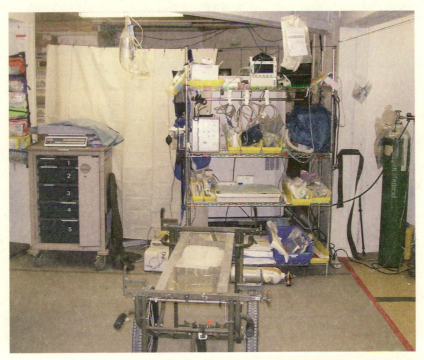

The trauma bay

As a general duty medical officer (GDMO), I will spend twelve hours on duty (0800–2000 or 2000–0800) in the clinic part seeing the small stuff, and walk the twenty metres to the trauma bays if anything serious comes in. I will be assisted by medics who do all the initial screening, take the history and perform a physical exam. We are located right beside the airfield, so the medevac choppers can land about fifty metres away. There is also a "Role 1 facility" a few hundred metres away, which is the equivalent of a general practice office. It does the long-term follow-up of wounded soldiers who remain in the theatre of operations, along with a myriad of other functions.

The MMU is a twenty-minute walk from my shack. Apparently there is a bus that makes the rounds of the place, but its schedule is unknown to anyone I spoke to, so everyone walks. One of my roommates, who has been here for months, has acquired a bicycle—smart. Right across the street from my shack is the American Gym. Although housed in a rough kind of Quonset hut, it is very well equipped with all kinds of exercise machines and weightlifting gear.

A block away from the gym is Old Canada House. This is the Canadian "social club" of my part of the base. It has a bunch of books, a large-screen TV and a patio. There are also Internet connections and phones. We are issued cards good for a limited number of minutes per week of phone and Internet use. There is also a New Canada House, which is bigger but has much the same amenities. It is on the other side of the base from my shack, so I have not had time to go there yet.

The social hub of the base is the boardwalk, a covered square that has stores and restaurants on two sides, though by "restaurant" I mean a place that makes food and sells it from a walk-by window. Be that as it may, you can get a Pizza Hut pizza, a Burger King burger and a Tim Hortons coffee here.

The centre of the boardwalk serves as a sports area. There is a ball hockey rink for the Canadians, and an area where the Brits and Americans can each play their version of football. You can also buy rugs and all manner of local crafts from shops that line the boardwalk. Apparently there is also a larger bazaar somewhere, but it only operates once a week.

The Tim's!

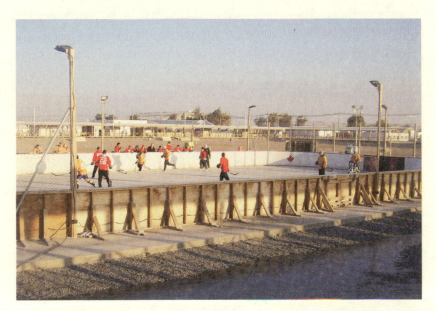

The ball hockey rink

Life here looks fairly good. Living conditions are far from miserable. The work should be interesting and challenging, and the team members I am with are fun characters (more on that later). All in all, not a bad way to serve your country.

NOVEMBER 17 | Getting into the Groove

Not a bad day.

Did my twelve hours from 0800 to 2000, then hung around as we got word that some ANA (Afghan National Army) troopers were coming in with shrapnel wounds from an RPG (rocket-propelled grenade). I got all revved up for my first combat-related cases, but the event proved to be both frustrating and anticlimactic. The only seriously wounded casualty unfortunately died in the medevac chopper.

It was very difficult to hear the medic describe the casualty's deterioration without being able to do anything about it. This death, like most non-instantaneous deaths in this war, was due to blood loss. This trooper could have been saved had he gotten to us an hour, maybe even thirty minutes, earlier.

None of the other casualties was seriously wounded, and only one of them needed minor surgery. The most interesting case, for me, came after that. Another ANA soldier accompanied the wounded, as he had been unable to urinate all day and was extremely uncomfortable. This was not the first time it had happened, and he had a lot of scarring from previous bladder surgeries. The word from the forward operating base (FOB) that had sent him in was that they had tried repeatedly to place a catheter in his bladder and had been unsuccessful. I took one look at him, at his degree of discomfort and the evidence of prior surgeries, and decided he needed a suprapubic catheter. This is a big, round metal "dagger" (think of a knitting needle, but twice as thick) with a catheter around it. You stab the patient in the abdomen, pushing the dagger in until it pierces the bladder. You then pull the dagger out, leaving the catheter in place to allow the urine to drain.

I brought over a little bedside ultrasound machine and took a look. This showed me that the bladder was much deeper than it normally would be, because of the previous surgeries and scarring. Not only that—the ultrasound machine showed it was HUGE—there was no way you could miss it. So I took a scalpel and cut *very* deep. A passing American specialist turned pale at this point, thinking I was killing the patient. Then I took the catheter and slipped it into the bladder on the first try.

The nursing staff and the other GDMOs, many of whom had never seen this procedure done before, were quite pleased. It was a good moment.

NOVEMBER 18 | Ramp Ceremony

A very bad day.

By the time you read this, the deaths of Master Corporal Nicholas "Nico" Beauchamp and Private Michel Lévesque will be old news. They were killed yesterday, along with an Afghan interpreter, when their light armoured vehicle (LAV) hit an IED. Some other Canadians were severely wounded. They arrived at KAF around midnight and were shipped out this morning to the NATO hospital in Landstuhl, Germany. This massive facility receives all wounded Coalition personnel from Afghanistan who require advanced surgical care, beyond what the MMU can provide. The treatment our soldiers receive in Landstuhl is world class. The doctors there have, unfortunately, had a lot of practice.

Today, we bid farewell to our fallen. This is done in a "ramp ceremony," so called because the dead are loaded onto a Hercules via the rear ramp after passing through a long cordon of their comrades standing five deep on both sides. As I was standing in the ranks, I did not take any pictures. The photos here were taken by the official photographer at an earlier ramp ceremony, in August.

The first photo is eerily like the scene I witnessed, as the dead in August also included a medic, shown here being carried by his fellows. And as in August, the person following the medic's casket was a woman.

A great sadness

Farewell

What made tonight's ceremony even harder to watch was that she was the medic's wife. They had deployed together, and they had gotten back from a three-week vacation together two days before he died. Now they were going home together.

Our ceremony took place at night, so it was even more haunting. It is difficult to describe the emotions one experiences during such a ceremony. There is great sadness, a healthy dose of fear, a determination to finish what we have begun. There is also a sense of belonging, a sense of having joined with all those Canadians who fought this country's wars and who stood in similar ceremonies. It will take a while to process all that.

NOVEMBER 19 | MasCal

MasCal is our abbreviation for mass casualty incident. These incidents are not as common as you might think. Our troops are fairly well protected, and most of the action involves only small groups of fighters. So truly overwhelming incidents only occur every few weeks. We had one tonight.

One of our FOBs had been attacked, and a lucky RPG hit had sprayed a group of our soldiers with shrapnel. Several of them were brought in by helicopter. Simultaneously, we received a number of ANA victims brought in after an IED strike on their vehicle, and a few civilians came in after having suffered gunshot wounds in an ambush just outside of KAF. As the "on-duty M.D.," it fell to me to coordinate the efforts of the medical and nursing staff from six different countries. In the end everyone survived, and except for one of our troopers and one of the Afghans, they will all be back to active duty eventually.

Describing the events of that evening would take a couple of pages. Suffice it to say that this was one of the most challenging and satisfying episodes of my medical career. It was hard at first to see our men all torn up, particularly the one who was worst off. I managed to shake that off quickly and get into my medical groove.

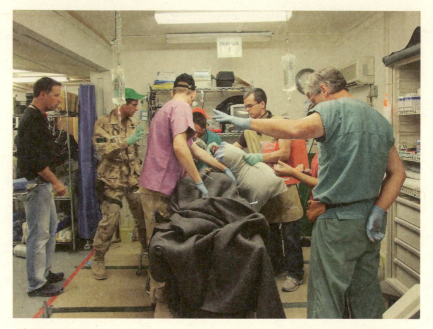

MasCal mob scene

It was also a busy night from an ultrasound point of view.* They have a bedside ultrasound unit here . . . but no one knows how to use it. So I ran from bed to bed checking patients for intra-abdominal hemorrhage and hemo/pneumo-thorax (air or blood in the chest). This made quite an impression on my colleagues, who have asked me to run a bedside ultrasound course for them.

The green hat in the first photo is worn by the senior trauma team leader, who supervises the entire trauma area, coordinates imaging (X-rays and CT scans) and prioritizes patients for the operating room.

The patient in the second photo is an ANA trooper. Before I deployed, I had the good fortune to find an Afghan woman (who had trained as a physician in the pre-Taliban era!) working in my hometown as an ultrasound technician. She taught me enough Pashto—the language of southern Afghanistan—to enable me to conduct my

---

* I am the director of Canada's national emergency ultrasound course.

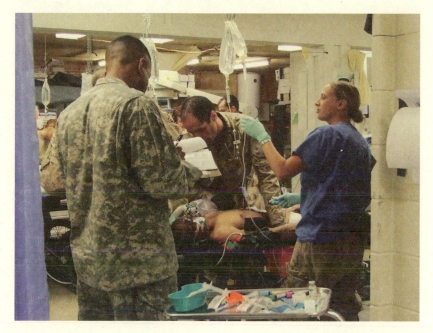

Gee tah sa wakaje darki?
Does it hurt to take a deep breath?

medical interviews without the aid of an interpreter. This is an invaluable advantage in emergency medicine, where the ability to "connect" immediately with the patient is vital.

NOVEMBER 20 | Last Working Day in Kandahar

It appears that my time at KAF is over—I am being bounced out to the battlefield.

The Canadian Forces is committed to providing the best possible care for its soldiers, so it tries to ensure that a doctor or a physician assistant (PA) is permanently stationed at all the FOBs. The nature of military medicine is that when things go wrong, they go very wrong. In those situations, you need a lot of experience and a lot of spare hands. This is sometimes difficult to do with the manpower we have.

My previous experience in the developing world, with the military and with the police, made me an obvious choice to fill one of the gaps at the FOBS.

This involves a quantum increase in the risk. Recognizing this, my commanding officer made it clear that his suggestion was a request, not an order. Given my background,* I had anticipated that something like this might happen. My wife and I had even discussed how I would handle such a request if it came. As I had promised her then, I called her to discuss it. She was not thrilled about the idea, but she agreed that this was a task for which I was uniquely suited and she approved of my going. So I said yes.

I'd be lying if I said I wasn't apprehensive (that sounds so much better than "scared shitless"). At the same time, I am happy to be going. I still feel a strong attachment to the infantry, even though my time with them ended twenty-five years ago. They have it hardest out here, going on foot-borne and vehicle patrols, searching for the enemy on the ground. They are the ones who have done most of the heavy lifting in this war: nearly three-quarters of our casualties have been in this branch of the service. They deserve the most support our army can give them. There may not be much to do on a daily basis at the FOB (I will be looking after a few hundred people by myself, rather than looking after twelve thousand as part of a team), but I am confident that I will like the independence and the proximity to the fighters. Most importantly, I will be right there if something bad happens.

---

* This is the second time I have been a member of the Canadian Forces. In the 1980s I served as an infantry officer. I graduated from the Combat Training Centre at Canadian Forces Base Gagetown, New Brunswick. This is the biggest base in the Commonwealth, with an area of 427 square miles (426 of which are swamp). I then served in an infantry regiment for four years. More recently, I have acted as medical adviser to the tactical unit (a.k.a. SWAT team) of our local police department for several years. I train regularly with them, provide them with advanced medical training, and go on the occasional call with them when my schedule allows. By the time I re-enlisted in the Canadian Forces, many of my old infantry reflexes and my shooting skills had come back.

This was my last day at KAF, so I spent most of my time getting my gear in top shape. I have been issued a *lot* more ammunition. Paradoxically, I find this both comforting and worrisome simultaneously. I am quite lucky that they have been able to find a chopper to fly me (and a bunch of other troops) to the FOB. This is far preferable to going by road and exposing oneself to the risk of IEDs.

I reported to the flight line at 1900, as ordered . . . and the transport gods (who had cursed my trip to KAF) acted up again. My flight was delayed over three hours, so I again got to sit beside a tarmac and sweat. The flight line was blacked out, so I couldn't read, and various aircraft (many of them ground-attack birds with incredibly loud afterburners) were continually taking off, so I couldn't sleep. Despite the fact that I was heading into combat, I was bored gormless.

Our ride, a Blackhawk, finally arrived and we piled in. Because air travel is so much safer than land travel, an effort is made to maximize the loads on each trip. We were packed in like sardines on this one. There was literally gear up to the roof. I could not put my seatbelt on, but that was not at all dangerous. I was wedged in so tightly that I would have stayed right where I was if we had crashed.

I am still having a lot of difficulty adjusting to the time change, still waking up at 0100. By the time I got on the chopper, I was completely baffed. It was crazy, but there I was, thinking to myself: *You're in a helicopter in an active war zone, headed deep into enemy territory. This is one of the most intense experiences of your life!* But all I wanted to do was sleep. I forced myself to stay awake for half the flight, then I conked out. They had to shake me awake when we landed.

I am actually writing this at 0300, because I have woken up yet again. Damn!

What constitutes an "adventure"? I think the most accurate description would be: something that is absolutely miserable while it is going on, but which gives you a great sense of accomplishment when it is over. By that criterion, Afghanistan, and more specifically FOB Lynx, is definitely an adventure.

Let me begin by telling you an anecdote from my pre-deployment activities. I was originally slated to deploy in the late spring of 2008. In late September, this was moved up dramatically due to various staffing problems in the Battle Group. This led to my zipping down to Toronto in early October to get all of my gear for the desert environment I would be working in ("arid camouflage," to use the military term).

Yours truly, in full combat uniform

Realizing that my life (at worst) or my comfort (at best) would depend on this gear fitting well, I took my time. I tried on several different pairs of boots and several different sizes of uniforms, and I jogged around the enormous warehouse to ensure that nothing chafed or rubbed the wrong way. When I was done, I pulled everything on and went to look at myself in the mirror. I was wearing the full combat uniform, frag vest, tac vest and my helmet. So I looked like the guy in the photo (me).

Out here in the combat area, this outfit might look kind of cool. But what I saw in the mirror that day was a guy in dumpy clothing who looked tired, dirty, uncomfortable, far from home and just miserable. And I thought to myself, *What on earth am I doing?* I talked about this with my wife

Home sweet home

that night, and we reflected on the fact that I was following in the foot-steps of many, many Canadians who have left family, friends and com-fortable surroundings to do their duty to their country and to humanity as a whole. Honourable, to be sure.

But I still looked miserable.

My second thought, upon seeing myself in the mirror, was: *Could this possibly get any worse?* The answer, even if no one was shooting at us, is of course a resounding *Yes!* Being in a forward area in a war zone brings together all the hellish aspects of summer camp, without any of the enjoyable activities that make summer camp worthwhile. So here I am, sleeping on a folding canvas cot about four feet from a medic who snores like a sawmill. He is well known for this. The other members of the medical team ensured they were in a room with no extra space, while the snorer was by himself in a large room. Coincidence?

All the Canadians here are packed into the remnants of an old school building. The walls are still solid enough to stop most of the shrapnel from the various things that are shot at us, but the roof is completely rotten. It is patched with duct tape in a number of places, and dust falls down on us whenever a tank drives by. Being unaware of this when I

Laptop about to get plastered

got here, I managed to place my laptop directly under a poorly patched hole and a big pile of plaster came down on the keyboard. I was able to get most of the plaster out, except for a piece that has fallen under the "U" key, rendering it unusable. As a result, the only way I can type the letter U is to copy it from somewhere else and paste it. The left "Shift" key no longer works either; nor do "Page Up," "5" or "Delete." Thankfully, "Backspace" is still okay.

As for the environment, we are on the very edge of a desert. The heat is not the killing 50°C of July and August, but the dust is overwhelming. And in a few weeks, the rainy season will arrive and transform all this into a sea of mud. There is the usual assortment of bugs, including monstrous spiders, scorpions and a thing that looks like a wasp but is (I swear) the size of a hummingbird, which I call a "Talibug." Did I mention the mice?

We also have a bank of computers for Internet access, something no modern army can be without, given the dependency of young people—like soldiers—on this modality. E-mail is as much of a part of these

We have running water . . .

. . . and laundry facilities

Ah, dinner! Another bag of...?

kids' lives as oxygen. Oddly, the computers are in a hallway off the main entrance of the building that is open to the elements—it will be chilly typing here in a couple of months! Then there is the fact that we are on a hill in a desert in Afghanistan. The Internet connection is via satellite and is tenuous. Also, we are only allowed twenty kilobytes of connection time per week, enough for a few dozen brief e-mails.*

And the food—having eaten institutional food so often in my life, I find most of the ration packs to be pretty good. Well, at least half of them. As we used to say at the Combat Training Centre: "Proud to be here, proud to serve. Every day's a holiday, every meal's a banquet. HUA!" (A note on military-speak: The cry of "HUA"—pronounced "hoo-ahh"—is not just a primal grunt of military enthusiasm. It stands for "Heard, Understood, Acknowledged." A commander might say it to end a briefing. Here, it would be a question: "HUA?" If the troops are clear on what must be done, they answer "HUA!" as an affirmation.)

---

* *Postscript, February 20, 2008:* Back at home now, it is difficult for me to convey just how important those twenty kilobytes were. Communication with home is everything to a soldier; I was constantly trying to devise ways to squeeze out the most communication from my allotted connection time, and there was a brisk market in extra kilobytes from those who, for reasons no one ever wanted to ask, made little or no use of theirs.

So what does rural Afghanistan, more specifically the Panjwayi district of Kandahar province, look like? FOB Lynx is on a piece of high ground that dominates the surrounding terrain, so the views are impressive. We're right on the edge of a desert here, so it's dry and dusty.

There are Taliban all around us, but there are more of them to the west than in any other direction.

And what do you think those green fields are all around us? Why, they're high-grade marijuana! Imagine that! I grabbed a branch of it for medicinal purposes.

Seriously, this army is quite strict about recreational drug use. Random testing keeps everyone clean. Even at KAF, the mission is "dry." Each CF member is entitled to only two 0.5 per cent beers a month— though I have yet to see mine. I'm not likely to for a while longer. Even the 0.5 per cent stuff is banned from the FOBs.

The one picture I can't show is one of the most impressive of all. The area we are in has no electricity, and we observe light discipline at night. That means we have completely covered all the windows, so no light shines through. White light, at night, carries very far and makes a

The view from FOB Lynx

Looking west—enemy territory

A whiff of medical marijuana

great aiming point. One of the results of this is that we are in an area of total darkness, with none of the light pollution that makes star-gazing so difficult for most North Americans. I have rarely seen Venus and Mars so bright; the Milky Way looks like a carpet, and it seems that there are shooting stars every minute.

One final point. Great news! I removed the U key from the keyboard with my bayonet and I can now type the letter U again, by pushing directly on the plunger thingy that is found behind the key. I would have given up on this diary otherwise.

Sunrise–moonset at FOB Lynx

NOVEMBER 25 | Working at the FOB

I work at the UMS, or unit medical station. Resources are limited, but I can do everything necessary to stabilize patients for the flight to KAF: intubate (surgically, if necessary—that means cutting the throat open if the patients are unable to breathe on their own and have facial wounds so severe that they cannot have a tube passed through their mouth into their lungs), ventilate, put in chest tubes (to raise a "collapsed lung"), stop major bleeding, rehydrate patients intravenously and stabilize spines and fractured limbs. We have a small range of antibiotics, but mostly we are geared to treat trauma cases (that is, people who are hurt, as opposed to people who are sick).

The wall of the UMS has an amazing mural created by Master Warrant Officer Jules Bérubé, the PA who ran the FOB Lynx UMS during an earlier Roto. It is entitled "Healing Hands of FOB Lynx." Beside the mural, you can see the traced outlines of many "healing hands," showing the hands of every medic who has served here in the past two years.

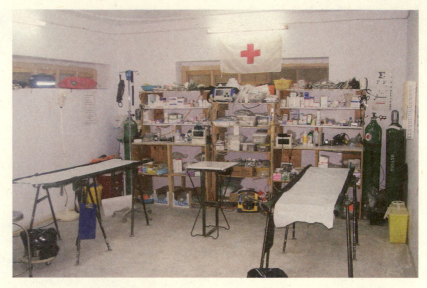

The UMS: rudimentary but effective

Life here is exactly what I was expecting: 95 per cent boredom and 5 per cent terror. It is remarkable how quickly one gets used to the "routine" of war. Even before I left KAF, I had gotten used to the sounds of rockets exploding and was, like everyone else, almost blasé about them. It is hard not to be, given the sequence of events. Once a rocket detonates (almost always somewhere on the perimeter of that enormous base), the danger has probably passed. A siren goes off, and we are supposed to put on our protective gear (helmet and frag vest) and head for the shelters—but most of us roll over and go back to sleep.

This is equally true here at the FOB. Ironically, one of the loudest noises here is our own 155 mm artillery shooting at the Taliban. These monsters can fire a massive shell tens of kilometres. Even though the artillery pits are about fifty metres from my room, they make the walls shake when they fire.

It may be difficult to understand that the excitement generated by us shooting at the Taliban or them shooting at us occupies only a small fraction of my day. Having had some experience of war beforehand, I was fully expecting this. The medics are comfortable dealing with most

The UMS mural and the "healing hands"

of the sprains, strains and aches of the troops. I consult on the odd case and do some preventive medicine, which mostly means ensuring that people are washing their hands after using the latrine. The rest of the time I am free to read, watch movies on my laptop (I brought a hundred DVDs with me) or otherwise entertain myself. After a decade in Canadian emergency medicine, it is quite something to work in a system which, on most days, has vast overcapacity. Of course, it will feel like exactly the opposite if we ever receive a large number of casualties here that the medics and I have to deal with on our own.

Now let me tell you about FOB Lynx itself and its role in the war. The enemy here is the hardest of the hardcore. The Taliban originated in Kandahar province, and this area—Panjwayi district—is one they have always dominated. Most of the Taliban training areas are just across the border in Pakistan, which lies thirty to forty kilometres south of us, making this district one of the main infiltration routes for fighters returning from rest camps, new recruits and weapons.

So what are we doing here, and how is it going? Over the past two years, we have pacified the eastern half of our area of operations, and we are now going after the other half. We started that process by building a small temporary outpost about three kilometres west of here, which we placed right beside the main Taliban cemetery in the district. This is the most direct challenge we can offer the enemy. We are telling them, in the clearest possible way, that they no longer control this territory. Not only will we deny them access to the population, we will also push them out of their sacred places. The Afghan government, with our help, now runs this part of the country. This has provoked an intense reaction from the Taliban: they attack our outpost nearly every day, occasionally several times in a single day.

This is exactly what we want. By using up their combat power in the boonies, the Taliban cannot mount many operations of much significance elsewhere. And they are definitely using themselves up. When they attack a FOB or our outpost, we retaliate with direct gunfire (rifles, machine guns, rocket launchers), as well as artillery and/or air strikes. Often, some of the Taliban attackers are killed or wounded.

We also do a lot of patrolling—our infantry goes out and hunts the Taliban on the ground. While contact with the enemy is only occasional here, this is where our skill-at-arms really shows. The Taliban are brave—no doubt about it—although they often step over the fine line that separates bravery from insanity. Some of them have been fighting for a decade or more. In spite of that courage and experience, however, the vast majority of contacts between Taliban and Canadian forces on the ground, where both sides are armed just with rifles and hand grenades, end in an overwhelming Canadian victory. It is exceedingly rare for our soldiers to get hit: the last time a Canadian was killed in a firefight with the Taliban (that is, by direct gunfire rather than an IED or roadside bomb) was over a year ago. But it is common for us to kill at least a few Taliban in most encounters.

A lot of this activity goes on at night, so our sleep is often interrupted by light shows created by illumination rounds. These are rounds fired from our artillery that are designed to detonate very high in the air rather than close to the ground. Instead of carrying high explosives, they have magnesium cores that burn very brightly. Their descent is slowed by a parachute, giving us a minute or so to check out the suspicious activity/noise/whatever that prompted us to fire the illumination round. We fire a lot of these from the FOB to help out the patrols and outposts.

The description in yesterday's entry of the combat here was not complete when I knocked off for the night. I still needed to describe the most significant aspect: improvised explosive devices, or IEDs, which have been the cause of most of our casualties. As fate would have it, I can now speak about this from direct experience.

47

We had sent out a patrol in light armoured vehicles, and they hit an IED on their way back to the FOB. Some of our men were severely wounded and landed on my medics and me within fifteen minutes of being hit. Forewarned of the seriousness of the injuries, we called for the medevac chopper before the wounded men got to the FOB. This gave me much less time to work on them than I normally have in civilian practice. Fortunately, the combat medics had done outstanding work and had already bandaged the life-threatening hemorrhage sites. They had also administered narcotics for pain control, so the scene was far less chaotic than it could have been.

With the help of the medics and other troopers, I managed to reevaluate all the casualties, ensure hemorrhage sites were controlled and airways were protected (only one needed a tube), check their breathing, get them fluid resuscitated (started four IVs myself, more than I have had to do in a single day since med school), perform bedside ultrasound examinations on them to look for hemo/pneumo-thorax (blood or air in the chest) and intra-abdominal hemorrhage (all negative), get their spines stabilized and get them warmed up.* In less than a half hour, they were all on a chopper bound for KAF. I don't think these soldiers will be back to active service, but they will all survive.

---

* Readers with experience in emergency medicine will be struck by the order of my actions. In civilian practice, we are taught to always follow the ABCs: Airway-Breathing-Circulation. But in modern war, we have learned that it is more effective, in terms of lives saved, to make the priorities C-ABC: Circulation-Airway-Breathing-Circulation. This is because soldiers who are not killed instantly usually die from exsanguinating hemorrhage (bleeding to death). The first priority is therefore to ensure that any obvious leaks are plugged.

This was easily the most intense medical experience of my career. Until it happened, I had not fully appreciated the degree to which rapid helicopter evacuation would limit the time I would have to do my work. This realization hit me full force when, just as the casualties arrived at the FOB, the combat team commander told me that the chopper would be there in about twenty minutes. There was also the unspoken, but nonetheless crystal-clear, expectation that I would not delay the helicopter evacuation of these men in any way. This did not change the fact that I wanted to ensure, as far as humanly possible, that I did not miss any serious injuries that could cause these patients harm during the transport. I had no trouble dealing with the wounds and the actual medical care—that's what I have been doing for the past fifteen years, and it's all quite automatic now—but I had to work faster than I ever have before. In civilian practice, I would have had twice as much time for a single patient.

The end result of this was that, as the helicopter lifted off, I was almost vibrating from the tension. Normal procedure at this point called for me to radio the KAF MMU to give the team leader there further information as to the condition of the wounded. This is exactly what takes place anytime an emergency physician transfers a patient to a surgeon: a verbal description of the case, including patient age, the mechanism of injury, the nature of the injuries, the care given to that point and the patient's response to same. I remembered to make the call, but I was so frazzled that the only thing I could mumble out was: "You've got three patients inbound, two of whom will need immediate orthopedic surgery."*

This brings us to the subject of soldiers and wounds. There are six fears that soldiers experience on the battlefield. The first five are dying, killing, sights and sounds, failure and the unknown. That may appear to be a fairly frightening and complete list. It often surprises people, therefore, to learn that when soldiers are asked which one they fear most, the

---

* *Postscript, February 2, 2008:* You can get used to anything. I did much better the next and subsequent times.

The unit aid station, after the wounded left

overwhelming majority—more than 90 per cent of them—will name the sixth: mutilation and disfigurement.* The reasons for this are complex and have a lot to do with who soldiers are: young men, to whom physical prowess is vital. The bottom line is that soldiers are affected as much, if not more, when their comrades are severely wounded as when they are killed.†

---

* Through the ages, a number of weapons have been designed to take advantage of this fear. These are weapons designed to maim rather than kill, such as some of the smaller land mines. Canadians can be proud that our country led the fight to outlaw these weapons through the Ottawa Mine Ban Treaty of 1997.

† *Postscript, February 9, 2008*: Our combat troops, though exceedingly well trained and competent, are not immune to this. Over the course of my entire tour, a small number of troopers came to me to ask for help sleeping. In all but one case, I managed to help them without resorting to drugs. I gave them advice about sleep hygiene (don't play video games right before going to bed!), but mostly, I encouraged them to talk about their fears. In these conversations, severe wounds loomed much larger than death.

The day's events affected me in two main ways. The first difficult part was completely unexpected. When the combat medic called to give me his report, I could hear our soldiers screaming in pain over the radio. You may find this odd, but in a lot of years of taking calls from ambulance crews, I had never heard a patient in the background. It caught me by surprise and left me feeling a little unnerved for a few seconds, mostly (I think) because I realized I was hearing my own troops. That dissipated fairly quickly.

The second way I was affected was much more predictable and longer lasting. Seeing the terrible leg wounds on my fellow soldiers and knowing their legs might be amputated made me very conscious of my body, particularly my lower limbs. I spent a fair bit of time tonight looking at my feet and moving them around, as if to reassure myself that they still worked. I expect that will last a day or two.

I had the same reaction during the Nicaraguan war, where I worked as a paramedic. While I was there, I cared for a soldier who had had both his arms blown off to the elbows by a hand grenade. I had been in the war zone for several months by that time and had seen injuries that were far worse, including seeing people who had been ripped apart by direct rocket hits. But this man's injuries affected me more powerfully than anything else I had seen. When he was brought in, I immediately thought: *He has lost his hands. He'll never paddle a canoe, rock climb or touch a lover again.*

What can I tell you? I was twenty-seven years old—those were the things that mattered to me then (come to think of it, they still do). For a few months after that, I had a recurrent nightmare in which my forearms just faded away. I would wake up sweating and panicking and using each hand to try to find the other. Not pleasant, but it went away.*

A last personal observation. I have been a little surprised to find that I do not want revenge against the Taliban for killing and maiming

---

* *Postscript, April 19, 2008:* I am doing the final wordsmithing on this diary before sending it to the publisher. So far, I have not had any nightmares about my experiences in Afghanistan. The upside of aging is experience and maturity.

our troops. It strikes me that it would be illogical to feel that way: they were having their little civil war here, and we came half way around the world to kill them. What were they going to do? Throw us a party?

What I *am* furious about is 9/11 (and the twenty-five Canadians who died that day). I don't buy the Taliban's story that they were unaware of what Osama Bin Laden was planning. Even if they weren't aware, I reject the notion that their code of hospitality precluded them from turning him over.

Even more than that, I despise the Taliban for what they are, for what they did and for what they continue to do to powerless people under their control. There is an interesting analogy to draw here with the work I do as doctor for the tactical unit (a.k.a. SWAT team) of our local police department. When the "Tac Team" goes up against a hostage-taker who is not of sound mind, they will go to extraordinary lengths to bring him or her down without the use of lethal force. And when lethal force has to be used to save the life of the hostage, these "hard men" take it very badly. A successful encounter is one that ends in an arrest or a psychiatric hospitalization, not a death.

I feel the same way about al Qaeda and the most radical elements of the Taliban. Their ideas are so diametrically opposed to anything I can imagine is rational human behaviour that there has to be an element of mental imbalance at work here. Be that as it may, they have to be stopped—and their hostages, the Afghan people, have to be released from their clutches. Their numbers and the degree to which they are supported make it necessary to use robust military intervention to achieve that. Going out regularly and killing these radicals gives time for the Afghans to build themselves up to the point where they can contain the threat themselves. When that happens, we can talk about negotiating with those insurgents whose motivation is more cultural or nationalistic. But there can be no negotiation with people as crazy as al Qaeda and the hard-line Taliban extremists, because negotiation begins with finding common ground. Halfway to crazy is not common ground. It's still crazy.

Our ambulance here is called a Bison, a wheeled armoured vehicle similar to the LAV. It has a crew of three: crew commander, driver and medic.

The crew commander of the FOB Lynx Bison is an infantry soldier tasked to this duty for the tour and not formally part of the medical team. The medic, Corporal Denis Bussière, nicknamed "Bubu," is quiet, unassuming and extraordinarily competent. For the trauma work we do, he functions at the level of a third-year resident in emergency medicine. Corporal Christian Demers, a reservist, is the driver. He keeps more to himself than the other two but is very easy to get along with. He is also very calm under fire. All in all, they are a fine ambulance crew. When our men get hit, they can count on these men to give them as fair a shake as any paramedic crew in Canada.

I could go on at length about the work these three men do, but that would be predictable. Let me instead share with you something I find absolutely fascinating about them. After having been out on patrol down a road potentially packed with IEDs or after having brought back our wounded to the FOB, what do you think these guys do to unwind? They fire up their laptops, which they have wired together, and they play war games. And not anything cerebral: you run around a virtual World War Two environment gunning each other down. It is true that I haven't played video games in quite some time, but I can't get over the realism of this one. When you shoot an opponent he cries out, blood sprays from the bullet hits and his body jerks from the impacts before crumpling to the ground. Initially, this was a bit shocking to see.

I was having trouble reconciling the consummate professionalism these men displayed on the job with what I considered juvenile behaviour while off duty. I worried at first that they were dangerously disconnected from what we were doing here. After a week with them, however, I realized that I was looking at a major generation gap. The oldest of them, the crew commander, is twenty years younger than I am. This is what they have always done to relax, probably since they were eight or

52

Crew commander

Driver

Medic

The Bison crew

nine years old. There is no reason for them to change just because they have gone to war. One only has to listen to them describe the way they felt when their comrades were killed to know that it is perfectly clear to them that the war is real.

Over the last few days, out of a desire to be a part of the team and also out of sheer boredom, I have taken to playing this game (*Call of Duty*) with them. The boys take great pleasure in gunning down their superior officer—something they have no trouble doing in about seven seconds. Bubu is particularly lethal, and revels in his ability to shoot opponents in the head at long range.

This is not the first time I have worked in a war zone. The others, however, were not nearly as intense as this one. The only things I was ever shot at with before were small arms: rifles and machine guns.* And yet, for all the high-tech weaponry and the heavy bombardments on both sides, this is a much more intimate war than the others in which I was involved. The war in Nicaragua, for instance, took place over the entire northern half of the country. Things are much more concentrated here. To better grasp the implications of this, a little geography might be helpful.

Since 2005, almost all Canadians serving in Afghanistan have done so in Kandahar province. The KAF base lies approximately ten kilometres south of Kandahar city. All of Kandahar province borders on areas of Pakistan where there is a large Pashtun population. This is the same tribe to whom the Taliban (almost exclusively) belong, giving them access to natural allies and safe havens.

Most of the fighting we have done for the past two years has taken place in the districts of Panjwayi and Zhari. Most of the Panjwayi is the uninhabitable Registan Desert (sometimes called the "Red Desert," presumably for the colour of the sand). Most of Maywand district—west of Zhari—is also a desert. The inhabited parts of Zhari and Panjwayi, a rectangle that measures only twenty by twenty-five kilometres, are the key battleground in the province. Starting in late 2005, we have gradually extended our control westward.

This has come at a price. From the hilltop observation post here at FOB Lynx, I can see the places where most of the Canadians killed in Afghanistan have died. This is well demonstrated by the interactive map at <http://www.cbc.ca/news/interactives/gmaps/afghanistan/>.

---

* They don't look very small when someone is using them to shoot at you. In Nicaragua I was hit in the left knee by only a *fragment* of an AK-47 bullet, and it still spun me around like a top. I thought I had dug it all out, but a piece of that bullet resides in me to this day, as I found out when I got an MRI in 2003.

Kandahar province, south-central Afghanistan

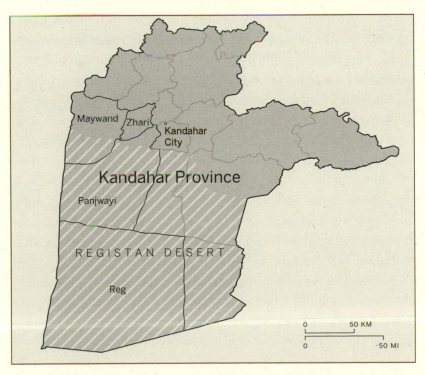

Maywand, Zhari, Panjwayi, and Reg districts, west-central Kandahar province

When you bring up this map, you will have to increase the magnification quite a bit to see the white markers representing the FOBs. The red markers, which show our casualties, cover them up.

More than sixty Canadians killed in Kandahar province and hundreds of millions of dollars might sound expensive for so little real estate, but that is the nature of counter-insurgency. Progress is measured not in territory gained but rather in attitudes changed. You can see that in spades.

Just fifteen months ago, in September 2006, the Canadian Task Force in Kandahar province launched Operation Medusa. This was the largest battle Canadian soldiers had been involved in since the Korean War ended in 1953. The goal was to establish a first FOB (FOB Leopard) in the Panjwayi district. Until then, the Taliban could operate up to the gates of KAF. Even early this year, FOB Leopard was still being regularly attacked by ground troops with small arms.

Although FOB Leopard remains the most heavily rocketed and shelled FOB in our area of operations, the effect of our presence there has been remarkable. Veterans of Op Medusa can't believe it when we tell them that the Taliban are no longer much of a threat in the nearby village. They had to fight their way in here, and it was a tough and costly battle. Five Canadian soldiers were killed, and dozens were wounded.

The work is far from over, but the progress is undeniable. The bush a few kilometres north of FOB Leopard, for example, is still bandit country. The Taliban launch their rockets and mortars from that area. The difference is that now much of the population in the district no longer lives in fear of them. New constructions go up near our FOBs because the population feels safe and knows that government services, most importantly schools, are not going to be easily destroyed if we are around. Eventually, the Afghans will have the confidence and the skills to stand up to the remaining Taliban on their own.

Because this is a counter-insurgency operation, our goal is to kill an idea: the concept of Taliban-style extremism. If we have to kill people in the process, so be it; but that is not the primary objective. This is the Taliban's home base, and they will keep coming back here until the population itself completely rejects them. When this war ends, there will still be Taliban in Afghanistan, just as there are still Nazis in Germany. It won't matter. They, like the Nazis, will be irrelevant to the lives of ordinary people because their ideas will have been discredited. We have to stay here long enough for that process to happen.

DECEMBER 1 | A Tragic Dichotomy

I have added up the total cost of all the vehicles, the artillery and the gear and salaries of the troops here and I get a figure that is well over $100 million. I think the money is well spent, because it allows us to defeat the Taliban by spending money rather than lives. The resulting contrast with the local population around FOB Lynx, however, is stark. The people here are very poor. There is no electricity and vehicles are a rarity, not unlike the many other places in the developing world where I have worked.

I have therefore been struggling with a dichotomy in my medical relationship to the local civilian population. We will do everything we can for civilians with war-related injuries. These are almost always generated by the Taliban practice of detonating their IEDs in populated areas, which kills far more civilians than it does Coalition soldiers.* Afghans wounded in this way are treated as well as our soldiers: air medevac and treatment at the KAF MMU. But all other health concerns are directed towards the Afghan national health service.

There is a sound reason for this. If we were to open our doors wide, we would quickly be overwhelmed and unable to care for our troops. It would also put us in competition with the local health care providers,

---

* When Coalition military action kills civilians, it makes quite a splash in the news back home. This is as it should be. These deaths are doubly tragic, and we need to constantly ensure that we are doing everything we can to minimize these incidents. But when, as is much more frequent, Taliban activity kills civilians, it barely gets mentioned. This is just bizarre, and it gives Canadians a skewed view of civilian casualties in this war.

which would be most unwise. It would put local people out of work, in an area desperate for employment, and create a very toxic dynamic where the local providers would be held up to comparison with us by their community. Even if the health care these people provide is not up to our standards, they need to be supported and developed, not undercut.

That makes it no less disheartening to reflect on what could be done medically in this area with even a fraction of what the war is consuming. Having said that, if there is no security, it doesn't matter how much health care you have. Safety and security have to come first. Remember Maslow's Hierarchy of Needs? Safety and security are preceded only by food, water, shelter and elimination (peeing and pooping, for those of you not in the health sciences). And with the Taliban in power, you can forget about health care. Remember: they denied women access to even basic, life-saving medical treatment.

So when I got a legal opportunity to bypass the rule, I jumped at it. On one of our patrols, we met a little Afghan girl who had been wounded some days before by an IED blast near one of our vehicles. The medic on the scene at the time had dressed her wound, and she was now asking us to take another look at it. I removed the by-now quite dirty dressing, cleaned the wound, applied some antibiotic ointment and redressed it.

It was a weird interaction all round. There I was in my frag vest and helmet, carrying my rifle and pistol and trying to make this child feel at ease. I placed my rifle against a nearby wall and lowered my "ballistic" (shatter-proof) glasses. I wanted to take my helmet off, but that is absolutely forbidden. There was an incident a couple of years ago where a Canadian officer removed his helmet to interact with a local elder, whereupon a Taliban who had infiltrated the village buried an axe in his head. This was a suicidal attack, as the aggressor was immediately killed by the officer's escort. Though the Canadian survived, he was left with severe brain damage. This has led to a hard "full-body-armour-always" rule for troops anywhere near danger.

The girl then asked me to look at her little brother, who had been burned quite badly on the neck about a year ago. He had thick scarring

The good sister

along the front of his chest and neck. His main complaint was that the scar tissue made it difficult for him to look up. There was an obvious place where one could have removed a band of superficial scar tissue and possibly improved things for him quite a bit. I radioed in and suggested we do exactly that. The commander of the FOB Lynx Combat Team was very empathetic. I could tell he wished it could be otherwise, but my request was denied.

I understand that we cannot be the local general hospital—we have to be ready at all times for a massive influx of casualties and we cannot raise expectations we cannot fulfill. But it was still hard to accept.

Although I had my camera with me, I felt uncomfortable taking pictures of these children. It felt a little voyeuristic. One of my escorts did not feel the same way, though, and quickly snapped this one. Notice that the little boy can't look up. Given that the picture-taking was unobtrusive (I didn't realize it was happening, and it looks like the children didn't either), I am happy to have a record of the event.

I thought you might be interested to know who is here with me. The Canadian contingent in Afghanistan is about 2,800 strong, but only a third of these are what you would call front-line combat soldiers: the foot soldiers of the infantry (the rifles-and-grenades-and-bayonets gang, the group I was proud to be a part of twenty-five years ago), the men who are in the tanks (which we call "armour") and the men who fire the cannons (which we call "artillery"—see the glossary at the front of the book). Also playing a vital role in this war are the men of the armoured reconnaissance (or recce, pronounced "rek-ee") troops and the invaluable combat engineers (who are primarily engaged in the anti-IED effort). Taken together, this is referred to as the Battle Group.

The core of the Battle Group is always an infantry battalion, which varies between six hundred and eight hundred men. You may be aware that it is the turn of the Québécois infantry to be here. They are the Royal 22nd Regiment. FOB Lynx is home to a company of that regiment. The Royal 22nd is known as the "Van Doos," a corruption of *"vingt-deuxième,"* or "twenty-second" in French (allegedly courtesy of Queen Elizabeth II's pronunciation).

Two weeks from now, December 14, is quite an important date in the history of this company. On that date in 1943, they were fighting in Italy and were ordered to take a prominent strong point called Casa Berardi, which was being held by elite German paratroopers. As the Van Doos fought their way towards the objective, the Germans managed to get on both their flanks and behind them, effectively surrounding the company. Surrender at this point would not have been dishonourable. The company commander, Captain Paul Triquet, chose a different course of action. He pointed out to his men that since there were enemy in every direction, they might as well keep attacking their objective. They followed him and took the strong point. By the time they did so, only fourteen men were still standing, out of eighty-one who had begun the attack. They then held the strong point against repeated German counter-attacks until they were reinforced. For his actions that day, Captain Triquet was awarded the Victoria Cross, the highest honour a Canadian soldier can receive.

The Van Doo Company at FOB Lynx today follows in that tradition. Half of the members of the company are paratroopers, and they have the best combat record in the battalion. They have also, unfortunately, suffered disproportionately. Half of the dead of this rotation come from their ranks. I have already mentioned Master Corporal Nicholas "Nico" Beauchamp and Private Michel Lévesque—see the November 18 entry. The company also lost Private Simon Longtin on August 19. These deaths have all come from IEDs—no mistakes or botched firefights, no one caught in an ambush. So I am hanging with some of the toughest and most competent troopers you can imagine. That's very reassuring.

DECEMBER 4 | A Question of Perspective

A quiet day, with a humorous note. At one end of our barracks is a tent where we eat. Most of the troops sleep tightly together and are not allowed to eat in their rooms, to help with vermin control. This "mess tent" has a television. The channel we watch is controlled by someone in Ottawa, which avoids fights over the remote. Most of the time they tune in some sports event.

This afternoon they broadcast an interview with Celine Dion. The troopers here, as you might expect of Québécois, were quite pleased to hear their idol and expressed considerable affection for her. But that changed when the interviewer reavealed that Ms. Dion's latest five-year contract would be worth . . . 300 *million* dollars. Things got even worse when Ms. Dion began to discuss what she found difficult about her life.

To say that the boys were nonplussed would be an understatement: I think we were lucky that the TV did not get shot to pieces. The troopers have been living . . . and dying . . . in conditions Celine could not begin to understand. I did not ask them how much they make, but as a medical captain, I make $320 a day. Infantry privates are certainly paid a lot less.

Here at the FOB you get the feeling that the severity of the issues that individuals will complain about is inversely proportional to the distance they are from the shooting. The combat team commander, Major

Patrick Robichaud, was howling last night as he recounted talking to someone at KAF and hearing this guy whine about how dangerous his job was and how difficult it was for him. The major asked him what he did, expecting to hear something like bomb-disposal or long-range reconnaissance. But no. He was some logistics loogin who had never been "outside the wire" (outside the confines of KAF). Major Robichaud, who goes out beyond the FOB nearly every day and who has been in vehicles that have been blown up by IEDs *twice* (with a third very near miss), got quite a kick out of this.

Addendum, December 19, 2007: As the combat team commander at FOB Lynx, Major Robichaud has a job that is unique in the history of warfare. He is an outstanding combat officer, the kind of leader who combines intelligence, forcefulness and a kind of preternatural grace. During the combat operations you will read about in later days, his voice on the radio was always calm, even in the midst of heavy fighting. It's a hackneyed phrase, but he really is the kind of man you would follow through the gates of Hell.

Normally, that would be enough. But in this war, he is also a diplomat, negotiator and community builder. These pictures show him doing something he does virtually every week. While the rest of the combat team kicks back at the FOB, he goes out with a small security detail and meets the local elders at a *shura* or council meeting. He asks them how we can better support the development of their economic infrastructure, their schools and clinics. He finds out whether our combat operations have hurt their crops or livestock (for which we will pay compensation). And he does all this knowing there are Taliban sympathizers, and even Taliban agents, in the room with him.

This is what it means to work with the people of Afghanistan. This is what it takes to be seen as the friends and supporters of ordinary Afghans, rather than just another foreign army. We can keep the Taliban at bay militarily forever, but until we build this country and its institutions up to the point where they are no longer a "failed state," we will never truly win. Major Robichaud's actions at these *shuras* are at least as important as his contributions in battle.

Meeting the elders at a *shura*

Partaking of Afghan hospitality

As a mark of respect for the Afghan culture, Major Robichaud sits on the floor cross-legged and partakes of the local food. More striking, to military eyes, he removes his helmet, ballistic glasses and frag vest. He leaves his rifle with the security detail waiting outside. He is virtually defenceless.

Think about the courage it takes to do that in a war where the enemy wears no uniform and has been known to attack Canadian officers with axes at these meetings.

You don't hear much about that back home, do you?

DECEMBER 6 | Great Balls o' Fire!

After dinner tonight we were alerted that some ANA soldiers were bringing in one of their members in acute distress (there is a bad pun in there, as you will see). They brought in a trooper who has been a problem patient since my first day here. This man was absolutely convinced he had something wrong with his penis. His history, physical exam and urinalysis were utterly normal, and he had no symptoms whatsoever other than "My penis is on fire" (no smoke or flames were visible, mind you). He kept coming every day, and we tried various benign things, but mostly I tried to reassure him. Nothing doing. Now he was screaming and thrashing around, and his buddies were freaked out.

Once again, I examined him and found . . . a rock-hard erection. What the hell? Seeing this, I asked the patient if he had taken any medication. He admitted that he had bought something from a local "pharmacy." Before Viagra, there was a drug called yohimbine, which did the same sort of thing. It occasionally led to something like this—the erection that would not die. This is called priapism, and I saw a case of it in my first year of practice. As the prolonged erection limits the flow of fresh blood into the penis, the blood already in there can start to clot and the penis can become ischemic (not get enough oxygen). This is very painful.

There are a couple of things you can do in this situation, but the easiest and least invasive is to apply cold to the penis. So I got one of those chemical ice packs we use for sprains and held it around the penis for about five minutes. He got soft, and he stated he felt much better. Off he went.

Before I go on, it is important to tell you that Afghan men are *incredibly* uptight about their genitals. Remember the patient at KAF into whom I put the suprapubic catheter? I had to use ProSed (put him to sleep) just to examine his penis, despite the fact that he was in agony. For this man to pull his pants down and allow me to manipulate his penis was very unusual. But so be it. His penis had reacted to the cold like a scared turtle, and he was gone. Another successful emergency medicine interaction.

Nope. He came back a half hour later, carried by his buddies, screaming again that his penis was "on fire." I checked. No erection, no flames. And now the other shoe dropped. Through his screams he stated that he had bought an "injection" which would cure him. We looked in his pocket and found a vial of ceftriaxone (a powerful antibiotic which can be used to treat sexually transmitted diseases). Now he started beating his chest, writhing so hard it took four men to hold him down, snapping his head violently from side to side . . . but he was speaking clearly.

I thought this display was not compatible with a real disease, but it was late, my other treatments had failed, I was dealing with a different culture and the vial looked legit, or at least sterile. So we started an IV and shot it into him. He immediately stopped screaming and said the pain was gone. Great! So get up and get out of here! Not gonna happen. Now he felt too weak to move! After ten minutes we sat him in a chair, whereupon he went completely rigid. He was one solid board of human flesh that only contacted the chair at the edge of the seat and the top of the backrest. At this point, I lost my patience. Cultural differences be damned, this guy was nuttier than a fruitcake! I told his buddies to take him back to his barracks. As they picked him up, he went completely limp and had to be dragged away. Seeing this, I told his sergeant that I never wanted to see this man for another genital complaint unless he had been shot in the balls.

Addendum, December 11, 2007: The patient turned out to be a total wingnut. The Afghan company commander discharged him from the ANA and sent him home a few days after the above events. This kind of thing reaffirms my faith in humanity. If our loonies are so similar, surely we can find other things in common as well.

DECEMBER 9 | First Combat Operation

Not all the combat activity is the outpost-and-patrol work described earlier. Occasionally something much bigger takes place. We went through such an event yesterday.

As mentioned above, the Taliban had taken to attacking our new outpost (see the November 25 entry) daily. As well, they would place IEDs on the road from FOB Lynx to KAF several times a week—sometimes mere hours after we had finished clearing it. This was a direct challenge to us, so it was decided to disrupt their operations in a major way. After much planning, we pulled together a number of Canadians, some superb British elements and some ANA soldiers for an operation to clean out Taliban concentrations we had identified in the area immediately west of here. Everyone headed out on foot at 0200, to be in position to attack

Heading out from the FOB in the dark

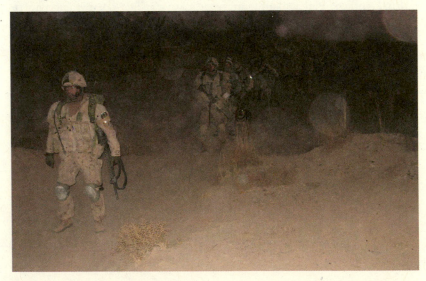

at first light. I spent the entire day with the command post, advising the commander on where our armoured ambulance could be best used and coordinating with the British medical team.

You will probably never hear about this operation in Canada. The media focus a great deal of attention on our lethal casualties but seem much less interested in victories like this one. We spent seventeen hours yesterday handing the Taliban one of the worst defeats they have had to endure this year.

They had recently reinforced the insurgents in our area with fresh troops from Pakistan, so even numbers were engaged. We had enormous technological advantages: artillery, tanks and aircraft. The Taliban had their advantages: perfect knowledge of the terrain and an ability to disappear by dropping their weapons and appearing to be civilians.

This made for an even contest, except for one thing: the skill of the Canadian infantry. Our foot soldiers spent most of the day dismounted from their armoured vehicles, as the terrain was often dominated by mud brick walls and *wadis* (irrigation ditches) that made all but foot-borne movement difficult or impossible. In spite of these challenges, our troopers were able to methodically drive the Taliban into killing areas where our artillery and air strikes were extremely effective.

While a lot of fire was traded between the ground forces, it was this "indirect fire" that did most of the damage. A noteworthy exception was the work of our snipers. Apart from providing outstanding reconnaissance from cunningly chosen vantage points, these men—among the best in the world at what they do—hit enemy targets at ranges that appear superhuman to me.* In the end, several dozen Taliban were killed and a large number were wounded. Taliban operations in the western part of the district are likely to be severely degraded for some time.

We managed to do this without scratching a single civilian. The Taliban routinely hide behind and among civilians, so this meant holding

* I am no slouch with a firearm. I qualified as a marksman in my pre-deployment training and once outscored all but one of the tactical unit officers I work with in a shooting competition. But what the snipers do is beyond Olympian.

LAV crew watching 500-pound bomb hit

our fire a number of times. As I said, we are here to kill an idea. There is no better way to achieve that goal than to spare those the Taliban use as human shields. We prove that we can achieve our objectives without resorting to their methods. Nietzsche said that when fighting monsters, one must be very careful not to become a monster oneself. We are doing a good job of that.

Just as things were winding down and all the troops were coming back to the FOB, I received a Taliban soldier who had been shot in the chest. After his capture, he had been carried on a stretcher by our troops for nearly three kilometres before they were able to link up with one of our vehicles. The place he had been hit was on the far side of a water-filled *wadi* and there was no way to get him across—the troopers carrying him had to go around the entire *wadi*. As a result, the total time from wounding to arrival at the UMS was over three hours. This patient showed exceedingly good timing. He crashed (from a tension hemothorax, or bleeding into the chest that collapses the lung) about two minutes after he had arrived.

As is typical of combat environments, the information I had received earlier was misleading. From the time the Taliban soldier had been captured and throughout his extrication, I had been told he had been shot in the abdomen. It was only when he was in the ambulance and about five minutes out that he was seen by a medic who reported that the wound was in the chest, that the patient's breathing was laboured and that a chest tube (which drains the blood out of the chest to allow the lung to re-expand) was almost certainly required. I had to scramble to get everything ready, but it went smoothly. The patient arrived on the verge of cardiovascular collapse (i.e., death), but I got the chest tube into him in record time. I drained about a litre of blood from his chest, and he improved dramatically. We got him ready for transport, and while we waited for the medevac chopper we made a point of telling him that we were Canadians, that we had taken good care of him and that he would be all right.

Afterwards, I could not help but reflect on the way he would have treated me had the situation been reversed. When I arrived at KAF, we were given a security briefing that covered a range of topics. As I alluded to in my introductory letter, "Why Am I Here?" the speaker ended his talk by describing what had happened to five ANA soldiers who had been captured by the Taliban in the area north of KAF a week earlier. The tortures these men suffered before being killed can only be described as medieval. It took a long time, and they died very hard.

Taliban soldiers who are captured by us are often terrified, because they think we will do unto them as they do unto others. This man was no exception. Whenever I would inject him with local anaesthetic, he would cry out to Allah . . . until he realized that what I was doing was reducing his pain, not increasing it.

Treating prisoners humanely is of course the right thing to do. But it is also the smart thing to do. Although a soldier may be furious with an enemy who has just tried, or even succeeded, in killing a friend, the best way to defeat him is to treat him well. Killing him just gives the other side another martyr. Caring for his wounds, feeding and sheltering him makes him doubt the cause he was fighting for.

When they see that we are not the monsters their leaders have told them we are, it is not unusual for these wounded prisoners to give us information we can use against their former comrades. Many of the Taliban foot soldiers have been brainwashed since childhood to follow whatever their *madrassa* (Islamic religious school) teacher tells them. But they can still reason. When they see us act in honourable and humane ways, they often begin to doubt the veracity of many of the things they have been told about us.

Before I close, I have to mention that there was something very odd about the Taliban prisoner. He was a native Pashto speaker, so he was from the area—not one of the Arab, Pakistani or Chechen partisans we occasionally run into. And yet, in this district where everyone is thin and the children I have seen have all been at least mildly malnourished, this man was . . . chubby. At least sixty pounds overweight.

We know that the Taliban get all their food locally, as the only things they bring in from Pakistan are weapons. The consensus here is that they likely extort the food from the civilian population. If this prisoner is any indication, the Taliban are eating a lot better than the people around them. In a way, this is good news for us. If the Taliban are eating better than the population, and at the population's expense, they are unlikely to be winning many friends. This is completely unlike an insurgency based on national liberation, but the Taliban are not fighting for a country. Like us, they are fighting for an idea—in their case, a sociopathic vision of the world.

DECEMBER 10 | Emergency Department Echo: FOB Lynx!

Those of you who know me professionally are aware that I designed a course called EDE, Emergency Department Echo. This course has known some success in Canada, having been taught to over four thousand Canadian physicians and having largely introduced the techniques of bedside ultrasound examinations to Canadian emergency medicine.

Having used EDE myself for nearly eight years, I've made it an

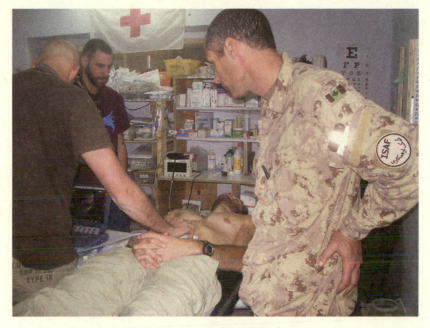

Emergency Department Echo demonstration

essential tool for my practice. I therefore arranged to bring a portable ultrasound machine with me from Canada. I have used it to evaluate our wounded (see the November 26 entry) and, in the case of the Taliban prisoner, for guidance to place an internal jugular central line (a large IV line that goes directly from the neck into the heart). The medics who saw that went wild and wanted to know how the thing worked, what the images showed, how to scan, etc. That was fine with me—I love to teach this stuff.

I only showed them cardiac and abdominal scanning, since that is all that is relevant to the work they do here. It may be several years before the Canadian Forces deploys ultrasound units down to the front-line combat medic level, but this is where it starts!

Interestingly, the Israelis use bedside ultrasound almost exclusively when they have a mass casualty incident caused by a bombing. You can't do a CAT scan on fifty people in fifteen minutes, but you can certainly check them with ultrasound.

I would like to tell you the story of the bravest man here, a Canadian captain attached to the Afghan National Army. I will call him Elmo, for reasons that will become apparent.

72

Let me tell you what he does for a living. He and the three Canadians he commands make up an OMLT—operational mentoring and liaison team—which of course is pronounced "omelet." The French translation is the even more unfortunate ELMO—*équipe de liaison et de mentorat opérationel*. So you get to be either an egg dish or a *Sesame Street* character. Either way, your acronym is the butt of constant jokes.

What this means is that Elmo is the "tutor" to a company of ANA infantry soldiers. For the past four months, he has taken troops we would consider barely trained and "escorted" them as they have gone into action repeatedly against the Taliban. As of our last combat operation, he has been under direct enemy gunfire more times than anyone else I know.

I will try to convey just how challenging a job Elmo has. Working with interpreters (the ANA speaks three major languages), he must explain modern infantry tactics to a group of very brave but poorly educated, often illiterate men. This is quite difficult. Using any weapon more complex than a rifle requires skills we take for granted, particularly mathematics, which the ANA recruits do not have. Communications and navigation equipment require even more baseline knowledge. On top of that, he can never be 100 per cent certain that his unit does not contain a Taliban infiltrator—not a pleasant thought to have in the back of your mind when walking around in the bush with armed men.

The OMLT logo

Elmo has managed to do this job exceedingly well, all the while retaining a remarkable sense of humour. I see him virtually every day, and he is always in a good mood. His men love him. And don't think he is someone who loves war. He is, on the contrary, the quintessential peaceful Canadian. This is his job, and he does it very well, but he can't wait to return to his wife and children. He supports the mission and the Afghan people, but he would much prefer it if it were possible to do so without actually being here. He understands better than most that this is not possible for now.

DECEMBER 12 | The Combat Team Mascot

No one knows where the little guy came from, but a few days ago a puppy followed one of our patrols into the FOB. He was immediately taken in by the troopers and made Combat Team mascot. This is a little odd, considering we are Combat Team Lynx—not a very canine affiliation.

After feeding the pup and giving him something to drink (he was starving and dehydrated when he arrived), the next priority was to clean him up. He smelled like he had spent a week in a sewer.

The Combat Team mascot

Tenderness in the midst of war

The soldier mopping the pup is as hard-as-nails as paratroopers come. Shortly after I arrived at FOB Lynx, he hurt his shoulder quite badly and I gave him three weeks off. Ten days later, he (politely) demanded that I allow him to go back to combat duty. It was very interesting to see him and his buddies showering so much affection on this pooch. I know it is a cliché to talk about soldiers seeking solace from war by showing tenderness when they can, but it is still neat to watch it happen.

DECEMBER 14 | "Hearts and Minds"* . . . But Not Abdomens!

Yesterday afternoon, we were advised that an Afghan man had come to the main gate of the FOB to inform us that his father had been stabbed and that he was bringing him to us. You will recall the rule we have about not giving medical care to the local population. There is an exception for life-threatening conditions.

---

* The expression "hearts and minds" comes to us from the Vietnam War. It is military-speak for the PR campaigns and aid programs aimed at convincing the civilians of a country in which one is fighting to align themselves with you.

The man arrived (via wheelbarrow), and Bubu the medic and I met him at the gate. He was in minimal distress but . . . he was eviscerated! There was a loop of small bowel hanging out of him. As often happens in these cases, the loop was now trapped outside the body: the abdominal wall had closed around the base of the loop, making it impossible for the bowel to slide, or even to be pushed, back in. When this occurs, the part of the bowel that is at the opening will eventually become swollen. This will cut off the blood flow to the part of the bowel that is outside the body. It will die, and the patient will die of infection after that. *Great*, I thought, *a clear-cut case of a life-threatening condition we can treat.* We loaded him into the armoured ambulance and brought him back to the UMS.

Once there, I cleaned off the extruded bowel as well as possible, covered it with a moist dressing, gave the patient some IV fluids and covered him with broad-spectrum antibiotics as well as tetanus prophylaxis and immunization. I performed a couple of bedside ultrasound examinations which showed that there was no internal bleeding. I then called the MMU and asked that the patient be transferred to KAF for definitive surgery. The on-call surgeon, a Canadian, completely agreed with me and was happy to accept the patient. Ditto the Canadian hospital commander. So I turned my attention to arranging a helicopter evacuation.

And here things broke down. My next call was to the KAF transport centre, which is *not* part of the MMU. The person taking the call asked me what the priority of the transfer was—specifically, how long the patient could wait for surgery. My options were 1 hour, 2 hours, 4 hours or 24 hours. The patient was completely stable at this point and I didn't want to cry "wolf" unnecessarily, so I said "24 hours." I thought that so long as the patient was in the O.R. by the evening, that would probably be okay. But the answer I got was: "24 hours? Then it isn't an emergency." I explained that it wasn't an emergency now, but it would be by some time that night if we didn't get him out. Nothing doing. Helicopter transport was denied.

This placed me in a real quandary. There were no vehicles in the village near FOB Lynx that could take the patient to KAF, and there was no way we could spare a vehicle ourselves, nor take the risk of riding down IED Alley (as the road to KAF is called). I called the surgeon back, and he told me I had no choice but to replace the intestines myself.

You have seen the picture of the UMS (see the November 25 entry). In no way does it resemble an O.R. We have masks and sterile gloves and drugs with which I can partially simulate general anaesthesia, but for instruments I have only small disposable scalpels and suture kits that have tiny scissors and forceps. We also don't have the best type of suture for this kind of work.

I explained the situation to the patient (laboriously, through an interpreter, as my Pashto was not up to this) and he agreed that we had to try. So I went for it. These three pictures show one of the more stressful experiences of my medical career. (Do I look a little tense?) Even when there is no choice but to proceed under very adverse conditions, a physician wants his patient to do well.

What we started with

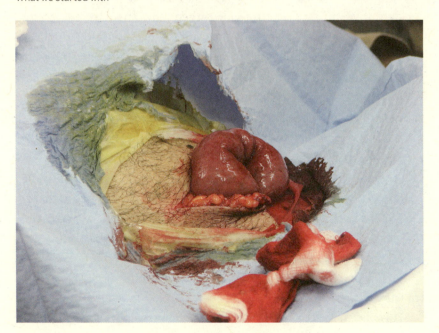

Looking for internal bleeding

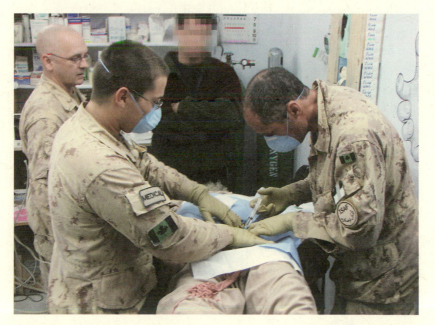

Operating with Bubu

The non-medical among you will have trouble understanding how difficult this was. The inner lining of the abdominal cavity and the sheaths around the muscles are tough, fibrous tissues that snap back after they have been cut and trap the loop of bowel on the outside. These have to be cut a bit more so that you can stuff the bowel back in. With the instruments I had, that was very difficult to do without cutting myself or harming the patient. Bubu the medic was my assistant on the operation. As mentioned previously, he is incredibly competent, and although he had never done anything like this before, he provided excellent help. The rest of the medics also rose to the occasion and immediately organized themselves into a competent O.R. team. In the end, I had everything back in and closed the patient up.

By the time we got all that done, it was after dark and there was nothing more that was going to happen that night. Believe it or not, I had to send the patient back home, telling him not to eat or drink anything and to return in the morning so that we could try again to organize transportation for him.

The problem now was that he still had a weakened area in the inner lining of his abdomen. This could lead to the development of a hernia, in which case the same problem of trapped and strangled bowel could develop, even if the skin stayed intact. In these cases it is often necessary to reinforce the inner lining of the abdominal wall with a synthetic mesh, to prevent such a hernia from developing.

There was also the chance that the original stabbing had hit some bowel other than the piece I had seen outside the body (which had no lacerations or other signs of trauma). If this was the case, a lethal infection could develop. Someone would have to open him up properly, decide if a mesh had to be installed and inspect the entire bowel to make sure it was unharmed.

The next morning, the patient returned as directed. To my great relief he felt fine, had minimal pain, did not have a fever and his wound looked good apart from some bruising. The sutures showed no signs of edema or strangulation.

The patient was feeling so well, in fact, that it took a lot of effort to convince him that he still needed another operation, but he finally agreed to go with an ANA convoy I had found that was willing to take him to KAF. Prior to his departure, I gave him more IV fluids and more antibiotics. I also provided him with a lengthy letter (addressed to the KAF surgeon) detailing the care I had given to that point. I called the KAF surgeon again to tell him that the patient was coming. All in all, a professional transfer of care. The surgeon congratulated me and told me that he would take over at KAF.

He never got the chance to see the patient. About two hours later, I got a call from my commanding officer at KAF. He told me that the patient, who now quite clearly was no longer an emergency, had been refused admission onto the base. He had instead been directed to go to the civilian hospital in Kandahar city.

I blew a fucking gasket. The care at the civilian hospital will be adequate, but that is not the point. I had started the case and transferred him to a Canadian colleague. It was inappropriate for us not to complete this process. Even if the patient chooses to go to the civilian hospital, which is far from a sure thing, the civilian doctors will not have had my report on what had happened and what treatment the patient had received. Physician-to-physician transfer of care is fundamental in our practice, and I feel angry and guilty that this will not have taken place. I asked the Canadian surgeon at KAF to try to contact the civilian hospital. He said he would try, but that would still be far inferior to a proper transfer of care. I am left to hope that my letter is read and understood by the civilian doctors.

Again, I understand the rationale for offering our services to the local population only in life-threatening cases, but it seems to me that this case met our criteria. Everybody here sees it that way, but at KAF I guess they see it differently.

DECEMBER 15 | Sex at the FOB

I bet that title got your attention. The reality, of course, is that there isn't any. Even back at KAF, where there must be a couple of hundred Canadian service women, things are utterly calm. There is almost zero flirting going on. The reason for this state of affairs (another bad pun, I know, I can't help myself) is that "fraternization" (which the military helpfully describes as "any touching of a sexual nature") is a crime, punishable by being charged and sent home. This rule—if you can believe it—also applies to *married couples who deploy together!*

Now I can imagine that some of you are thinking: "If I was there, I'd jump into bed with the first person who would have me. I'd get laid *and* get to go home—what a deal!" Obviously, career military people see it a bit differently.

I have not wanted to pry too much into the rationale for this rule, but I am aware of one interesting statistic. You will recall that during the first Gulf War against Iraq (1990–1991) Canada did not participate in ground combat. Only our pilots were in action against the enemy, and none of them got hurt. So what do you think was the most common medical reason for which Canadian Forces personnel were sent home? The answer is . . . pregnancy.

This rule, like all rules, is enforced more stringently at KAF than out here. So the FOB has been all agog for the past two days because one of our support personnel has somehow managed to get his wife, who works at KAF, deployed here for a few days. They seem to be going for several long walks every day. And while our OPS can see every inch of terrain leading up to the FOB, it is fairly certain that there are a few blind spots on the FOB itself where one . . . or two . . . people could hide.

For a while, at least.

Not that we're looking for them. Much.

What happens at the FOB . . . stays at the FOB.

DECEMBER 17 | Second Combat Operation

Like the first combat operation I described in the December 9 entry, I am fairly certain that you have not heard of this operation either. That is unfortunate, because it was as close to perfection as a combat Op can be. Whether or not Canadians agree with our mission here, they can be very proud of the skill and professionalism of their soldiers.

After our forces mauled them on December 8, the Taliban made a lot of noise about taking revenge. A lot of this had to do with saving face. After the kind of defeat they suffered nine days ago, it was vital for them to show the population that they were not a spent force. Rather than wait for this attack, we brought the fight to the Taliban. A key principle of war is to maintain the initiative and make the enemy react to you.

Yesterday's Op was a textbook "hammer and anvil" operation. It was executed in the eastern part of Zhari district (see the maps in the November 30 entry). Once again, we teamed up with the British and the ANA. This time, the Canadians snuck into positions before first light and waited. When the British and ANA started their push, the Taliban found their escape route cut off by the Canadians, leaving them nowhere to flee but out across open ground. Once the enemy troops were visible and away from civilians, we cut them to pieces, mostly from the air, although the artillery had some good hits as well. There were dozens of confirmed kills. There were no civilian or Coalition injuries.

Having described two battlefield successes, I feel it is necessary to talk about something called the Senlis Council. This NGO was formed in 2002 to argue for a "harm-reduction" approach to drug abuse problems.

Although they started with a global agenda, the Senlis Council are now focused on Afghanistan and its opium (currently the source of 90 per cent of the world's heroin). They argue that if Afghan peasants could be weaned from the drug trade, it would go very far towards stabilizing the country. To do this, they have proposed a project called P4M: Poppies for Medicine. Under P4M, donor countries would buy the opium directly from the farmers and have it processed at the village level, in Afghanistan, into morphine. This could then be sold in the West and, at subsidized prices, in the developing world.

The Senlis Council describe three distinct benefits to this approach.

First, the Taliban would lose the major source of their funding. They have always been heavily reliant on the drug trade to finance their activities. With breathtaking hypocrisy, the Taliban had issued an edict while they were in power stating that while drugs were forbidden under Islam, it was acceptable to make them for non-Muslims. They then extended this hypocrisy to their own people, calling the tax they imposed on opium farmers a *zakat* and setting it at 20 per cent. The Koran does direct Muslims to pay *zakat* to religious authorities, but it is set at 2.5 per cent and is to be used to care for the poor.

It was therefore a surprise when, in 2000, the Taliban outlawed the planting and harvesting of opium. They enforced this in their usual brutal manner, and opium production in Afghanistan fell by over 98 per cent.[*] They were so successful that, in one of the supreme ironies of the war, the United States gave them millions of dollars as a reward for having contributed to the "War on Drugs."

The irony doesn't end there. We now know that when the Taliban issued their decree to cease poppy production, they had huge reserves of opium already processed. The only reason they halted production was to keep the price of opium high while they got their stockpile down. It is certain the Taliban planned to allow poppy farming to restart when their stocks ran out. It was no concern of theirs that the farmers saw their livelihoods destroyed in the intervening time.

The second benefit would be for the Afghan population. They would be able to continue farming a high-value crop they already know well, but in a safe and officially supported environment. Large numbers of people not involved in farming could be employed processing the raw opium into morphine. Not only would this help alleviate the grinding poverty that fosters the development of extremism, it would also bind the population to the government by the tightest bonds possible: those of economic self-interest.

Finally, there are the subsidized clients in the developing world who would have access to inexpensive analgesia.[†] All in all, this is an excellent idea that should be implemented as quickly as possible.

---

[*] Of course, heroin (which is made from opium) continued to be readily available on the streets of Europe and America during this time. The demand for drugs is such that shutting down production in one area merely stimulates production elsewhere. Until the demand decreases, there will always be a supply.

[†] Some of the people who oppose P4M are completely out to lunch about the adequacy of pain control in the developing world. The 2007 report of the International Narcotic

The main reason I am bringing this up is that the Senlis Council recently issued a report that I feel is completely wrong about the military situation here. This has apparently been getting a lot of play in Canada lately. The report gives a very negative outlook for the future of our mission in Afghanistan and predicts that there is a good chance the Taliban might take Kabul in 2008. I don't claim to have more than a ground-level view of a small part of the war, but it is impossible to reconcile what I have seen here for the past month with such a claim.

To be able to take Kabul, the Taliban would have to mount an attack with several thousand troops, as they did when they first took the city in 1996. Even here in the restive south, their home base, they have been reduced to never gathering in groups larger than twenty fighters. Any troop movement larger than that gets detected and attacked, with devastating results.

I agree that we are a long way from having stability in Afghanistan, but the Taliban are unable to launch anything more than hit-and-run operations. Look at our casualties. They are almost all caused by IEDs, which we run into while chasing the Taliban or interdicting their movement. IEDs are the weapons of a guerrilla group on the run, not of an army on a victorious advance.

When I was at the Combat Training Centre in the late 1970s, we were taught that counter-insurgency requires a force superiority of ten to one. The insurgents can hide as long as they want and only strike when it suits them. The other side must maintain troops over a broad area to be able to counter the insurgents any time they surface.

Control Board (a quasi-independent branch of the UN) states: "The often expressed view that there is a global shortage of opiates for medical purposes, which is often used to advocate legalization of opium poppy cultivation in Afghanistan, is not based on hard facts." But the board's own data, published along with the report, shows that North Americans consume *one thousand times* more medicinal morphine per capita than Africans do. Patients in the developing world are suffering on a biblical scale. If they do not use much morphine, it is because *they can't afford it.* Anyone who has worked in the developing world knows that. The health care system in Africa alone could use all the morphine that Afghanistan could produce. To claim anything else is utterly moronic.

Let's put that in the Afghan context. Here in Kandahar province, the very home turf of the Taliban, less than a thousand Canadian combat troops, with ANA "mentorees," the odd helping hand from the Brits and American air support, are able to chase the Taliban into the ground.

You are probably aware that some of our NATO allies restrict the use of their troops to areas where there is virtually no Taliban activity. If they were ever to redeploy their forces here, the Taliban would find it very difficult to operate at all.

There is one last observation I would like to make, one that students of insurgency war will immediately understand. If you look at insurgencies in the past, their record is abysmal. The vast majority have failed. That is hardly surprising: dominant powers are extremely difficult to dislodge. The insurgencies that have succeeded, regardless of whether their motivation was ideological, nationalistic or religious, have all had one thing in common. *Just before they win, they suffer enormous casualties.*

Take the Nicaraguan revolution. It had grumbled along for twenty years, during which time rebel losses were usually a few dozen a year, with a couple of years where they lost a few hundred. In 1979, in the two months leading to the overthrow of the Somoza dictatorship, rebel losses were over 50,000. This was at a time when the total population of Nicaragua was only three million. That would be like Canada losing 550,000 in sixty days. To put that in context, remember that we suffered 40,000 deaths in six *years* during World War Two.

Somoza pointed to the huge losses the National Guard (really his private army) was inflicting on the rebels and felt reassured. That was a mistake. When rebel losses go that high, it means there are a lot more of them. The population as a whole has decided to ally itself with the insurgency. When that happens, victory for the insurgency is not far off. The capacity of the ruling regime to kill large numbers of people remains intact, for a while, and the insurgents suffer greatly, for a while. But the end is near.

Taliban casualties, even from major victories of ours like the two operations I have described, are in the dozens. There just aren't many of them out there for us to kill. They can cause a ruckus by planting bombs, by staging hit-and-run raids on civilians and the hapless ANP and by intimidating people in isolated villages at night. That's all they can do. To think that they can mount a viable military offensive against Kabul is absurd.

As long as we stay here, this is a war the Taliban cannot win and one the Afghan government cannot lose.

DECEMBER 18 | On the Road

This was my last day at FOB Lynx. Although it was initially planned that I would return to KAF at this time, I was asked yesterday to cover another FOB (FOB Leopard, northeast of FOB Lynx) for the next month, to allow the PA there to go on leave. He had been at the FOB since August.

The distance between the two FOBs is less than ten kilometres, so helicopter transport was not going to happen. That meant I would have to join a convoy and go by road. This is a lot worse than going cross-country on an attack, since IEDs are almost never placed out in open fields but instead where there is a high probability of a vehicle passing

Husky mine-clearing vehicle

LAV from the bow

over them. The most dangerous thing you can do here is go down a road. And the road we would have to take was recently acknowledged to be the second-most-dangerous road in the world (a road in Iraq took first place).

It gets worse. Since it had been some time since anyone had driven on this road, the likelihood of IEDs was considered extremely high. The convoy making the trip was therefore a mine-clearing mission. This is an operation run by the engineers to detect and destroy any IEDs that have been placed along our access roads. Our convoy was therefore led by a Husky mine-clearing vehicle. This vehicle is purpose-built to withstand mine blasts. The shape of the hull is accentuated, so the explosive force is diverted away from the crew compartment. These things are designed to be blown up, and they have been a number of times. Although no one has ever been seriously hurt in one of these, it is still quite understandable that the driver of our lead Husky put a sign on the back of his vehicle that read: "Do all jobs SUCK . . . or just mine?"

There were also a couple of LAVs with infantry troops for security, an armoured bulldozer and a couple of pickup trucks with ANA soldiers

The aft starboard sentry

for added security and to interact with the locals. The commander rides more or less in the middle of the convoy, and that's where I was loaded.

While it was certainly comforting to have all of that mine-detection equipment and expertise out in front of me, this was negated by the fact that we had to clear the road all the way to the outpost west of us before heading east to FOB Leopard, effectively tripling the distance and the time we would be exposed to attack. This is likely to be the longest road trip I will undertake through an area of high Taliban activity. The troops do this regularly and are either used to it or very brave or, most likely, both. For myself, I slept poorly till about 0400 and not at all after that. I don't think anyone could tell how I was feeling—I still have a lot of pride, maybe too much—but I got fairly quiet.

I spent my last evening at FOB Lynx packing and going over every last piece of my gear, particularly my weapons, to make sure everything was as "tight" as possible. I sterilized my "camel bag" (a four-litre water container that goes on your back) and filled it to the brim. I double-checked every pouch on my tac vest, making sure that all my ammunition and medical gear was snug, yet easily accessible. And I don't think my rifle and pistol have ever been cleaner.

The seriously wounded soldiers I have treated were all injured by IED strikes on vehicles. While waiting to board my LAV, I kept seeing their severe leg wounds, some of which had led to amputations. My awareness of my lower limbs, which had gone back to normal a couple of days after the last IED strike, became exquisite again.

We left FOB Lynx right after breakfast. As the vehicles crossed the gate, everybody was "locked and loaded": weapons fully loaded, a round in the breech; a flick of the safety, and we are ready to fire.

I took my position in one of the rear hatches of the LAV. The routine here is to scan your "arc" more or less continuously, using the scope on your rifle to closely examine anything that looks suspicious. As I was the aft starboard sentry, my arc was 3 o'clock to 6 o'clock (12 o'clock being the front of the vehicle).

For most of the trip we were in flat, open terrain. Potential ambush sites were at least two hundred metres away. The fire would be less accurate, and we would have a few seconds to react. At other times, as shown in the first photo, there was good cover all the way up to the road.

As unpleasant as it was to be driving down the road worrying about hitting an IED, it was worse when we were stopped in these areas, something we had to do regularly to let the IED-detection team do its work. An ambush from this proximity, although suicidal, would almost certainly hurt some of us as well. One of the places we stopped was right beside a bend in the road where one of our men had been killed by an IED several weeks earlier. It was a sobering and frightening moment.

The road to the outpost took us by the Taliban cemetery I mentioned in the November 25 entry. Everyone lying there had been put in the ground by us. I was happy they were dead, but you can't help but reflect on the wastefulness of war in places like this. I also felt that way in 2004, when I went to Normandy for the sixtieth anniversary of D-Day. I spent a bit of time in a German cemetery, asking the German dead: "Was it worth it? Would you do it again, knowing that you would

Good cover—not always a good thing

A Taliban cemetery

be killed? Knowing what a monster you had supported?" Maybe one day I will walk in that Taliban cemetery and ask the same questions.

We spent an hour at the outpost, resupplying the troops there. We then went back the way we came, past the turnoff to FOB Lynx and on to the east. As we got close to the village that sits beside FOB Leopard, the scene became a cliché: heavily armed Western troops in armoured vehicles riding through an area crawling with kids—all of them dirt-poor and begging for handouts.

We didn't stop to interact with the children, nor did we give them anything. Anyone who has been to the developing world knows that giving kids handouts encourages the worst kind of dependency. Here in Afghanistan, there is an even better reason.

On September 18, 2006, Private David Byers, a soldier from Espanola, Ontario (just outside my home town of Sudbury), was killed not far from here. He died, along with three other Canadians, when a Taliban suicide bomber on a bicycle drove into them while they were feeding Afghan children. There were twenty-seven Afghan casualties that day, most of them children.

A village near FOB Leopard

Getting to FOB Leopard confronts the visitor with a classic third-world conundrum. Although FOB Lynx is just a few kilometres from here, the contrast between the villages near each FOB is dramatic. Near FOB Leopard there are paved roads and lots of vehicles, and about half the village is electrified. I would bet dollars to doughnuts the folks in the village near FOB Leopard think the people near FOB Lynx are a bunch of hicks. Human nature dictates that they would.

I took a picture of the village from a spot just outside the perimeter wire of FOB Leopard. The foreground of the photo shows a large primary school. What I can't show in one still photograph (though it came out very well on video) is the reason the school is there: we have heavy machine guns sited to watch over the school. You could not ask for a better metaphor for this mission. We guard the schools; the Taliban try to destroy them.*

In the end, we arrived at FOB Leopard without incident. We didn't find any IEDs. This does not mean there weren't any, but it greatly reduces the risk for those who will use the road after us.

It was an interesting day from a sightseeing point of view, to be sure. It was also a long, uncomfortable day, with more than its fair share of anxious moments, at least for me. One feels exceedingly vulnerable on the roads of Panjwayi district, particularly when on a mine clearing operation. As I stood in the LAV's hatch watching my arc, I found myself wiggling my feet around, almost unconsciously. It probably looked like I was working out a cramp. What I was really doing was enjoying how good it felt to have my legs working properly. I was hoping intensely they would feel the same at the end of the day.

Like aircraft landings, any mine clearing operation you walk away from is a good one.

---

* *Postscript, June 30, 2008:* Here are some statistics every Canadian should know. In 2007, the Taliban forced the closure of 300 schools and burned or blew up 130 others. They also killed 105 students and teachers, almost all of them female. See Nancy MacDonald, "A School of One's Own: A B.C. Student's Quest to Get Young Afghan Girls Like Her Educated," *Maclean's*, June 9, 2008, 54(2), 121–22.

End-of-trip "hero shot"

DECEMBER 20 | FOB Leopard

This is where I will be working for the next month. The photograph on the next page shows my team. Let me introduce them.

Master Corporal Gino Tremblay (centre), the crew commander, is one of the most solid soldiers you will ever meet. Absolutely unflappable, always quiet and calm, an excellent combat leader. He is an ex-infantryman who has been with the medical corps for several years. He is an outstanding medic in his own right. He is also one of the most insightful enlisted men I have met here. He knows the history and culture of Afghanistan and understands our mission here perfectly.

Corporal Michael Langlois (right), the medic, is amazingly good at his job. As with Bubu at FOB Lynx, working with him is like working with a senior emergency medicine resident. He is also a bit of a prankster, which helps keep everybody loose.

Corporal Frank Vachon (left), the driver, is a reservist who is a trucker in civilian life. He is the archetypal gruff, heavy-smoking man, but he is very hard working, sharp and completely dependable.

My team at FOB Leopard

(Before you think that I make hasty judgments, you should know that I wrote the above descriptions after being here for three weeks and going through some tough times with these men, as you will see. It just fits better here.)

There is also some infantry here from the Van Doos, as well as some ANA with OMLT mentors. As with FOB Lynx, the base is on a piece of high ground, giving us even more spectacular views.

I live in a bunker made of "Hesco Bastions," gigantic sandbags filled with gravel. The roof is made of wood beams overlaid with concrete, so we are quite well protected. No one has ever been killed inside one of these things.

The bunker is a lot roomier than the one at FOB Lynx. The floor is made of wood on top of the ubiquitous gravel of the FOBs. All my stuff is laid out in dividers (it was crammed under my bed and on a single shelf at FOB Lynx).

The Internet access, though still quite limited, is in a shack. The shelf for the computers is set at about shoulder height for a seated person.

The view from Hilltop OP

Apartment 1, Hesco Bastions Manor

The bunker at FOB Leopard

After ten minutes you can't feel your hands because the blood has run out. At least we are protected from the elements. The "open-air" concept was getting hard to take at FOB Lynx . . . and it's getting colder!

The food here is amazing. The FOB Leopard cooks are known for being the best and most resourceful kitchen team we have in Afghanistan. They make breakfast and lunch every day, and it is always good (there is even a *salad bar*). As an added bonus, because their bunker is next to ours, they invite the medical team over when they make dinner for themselves—we eat like kings!

There are *two* fully operational "shower cans." These are things that look like cargo containers from a ship. Inside, they have been rigged up as five-shower washrooms. Connect them to a well and you're good to go. The water supply is limited, so we take "navy showers": get wet, turn water off, lather up, turn water on, rinse, turn water off. It's short, but it's a lot better than standing under a jerry can. Hot showers in the field! Excellent!

This FOB is home to the tanks we have deployed here. The tankers are drawn from units all over Canada, giving the base a pan-Canadian

A shower can

Leopard tanks firing

feel. They are equipped with Leopard tanks, state-of-the-art machines armed with a 120 mm cannon and remarkably effective target acquisition systems. The Leopard tanks shown in the photo were out on a "range day" (yes, tanks go to shooting ranges to practise, just like the local rifle club . . . only different). In combat, three tanks would never be so close to one another.

Few people have ever seen what a Leopard tank can do to a target, and I am struggling to find a way to describe the firepower, mobility and relative invulnerability of these beasts. I will try to do this with an analogy. Consider what the Taliban have in their arsenal: rifles, machine guns, mines and light-to-medium artillery. That is roughly the same as what the Germans had at their disposal on the beaches of Normandy in 1944. If you could take the Leopards at the FOB and put them ashore on D-Day, the 175,000 men the Allies sent to hit the beaches could have taken the day off. Not only is the Leopard's capacity for destruction truly awesome, it is also very heavily armoured—Leopards were made to take on the most modern tanks in the world. The stuff the Taliban throws at them has very little chance of wounding the crew.

DECEMBER 21 | FOB Leopard: The Downside

There is only one downside to serving at FOB Leopard, and it is summed up nicely in the welcome sign that hangs beside one of the other bunkers: "Proud to be rocket free for XX days."

This place has the dubious distinction of having had the most rocket hits of any FOB or outpost in Afghanistan. After IEDS, these 107 mm and 122 mm rockets are the things we fear most, because they have the largest warhead of anything in the Taliban arsenal. They make a hissing noise as they go by. This is good to hear, as it means the rocket is already moving past you.

As they had done at KAF, the Taliban celebrated my arrival yesterday, this time with a mortar round. Fortunately, though unnervingly, these bombs travel slower than the speed of sound. Their arrival is announced

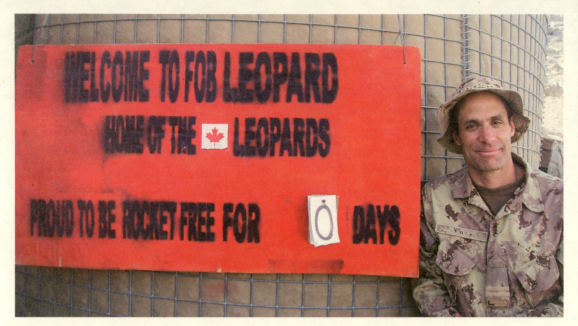

FOB Leopard welcomes you!

by a high-pitched whistling that you learn to recognize very quickly and that I recalled from my infantry days. This gave me a few seconds to hit the dirt before the mortar impacted. Unlike that first rocket at KAF, I can tell you exactly where this one hit. Mike the Medic and I were caught just outside the bunker when it came in, and we did not have enough time to make it to the entrance. We lay flat on the ground and glued ourselves to the bunker wall, hoping mortar would not land on our side of the structure. No one here is blasé about these weapons.

When I was asked why FOB Leopard was the subject of so much high-explosive attention, it was explained to me that various Taliban specialize in different weapon systems. The ones around this FOB are "rocket men." Great.

If you look carefully at the sign in the photo, you will see that there is a hook for the "tens" column (that is, when you get over nine days rocket-free). I asked around, but no one knew where the numbers for that hook were. Apparently, they don't get used very often. Now, that's comforting. As a result, almost every installation of any consequence here at FOB Leopard is surrounded by concrete barriers, the same ones that make up the rocket shelters at KAF.

As mentioned in the November 25 entry, the rockets don't carry that much high explosive. The main danger is from the shrapnel (metal pieces from the rocket itself, stones propelled by the explosion, etc.). The concrete protects you effectively from this.

The pair of washroom photos show the effect of a rocket on a shower stall. (From yesterday's entry, you will recall that these things are made of heavy metal.) The first photo shows where the shrapnel came in. It crossed the room, shattered the mirror on the other wall and went right through the metal side of the shower bunker on the other side.

The observant among you will notice that two pieces of shrapnel entered the shower, but only one crossed the room to the mirror. The other piece struck and killed an Afghan interpreter. Though this occurred some weeks ago, the damage has not yet been repaired. A real morale booster, that.

Because of that death, some of the men never shower in that stall. I, on the other hand, make it a point to always shower in the same stall in which the interpreter was killed. It's pure statistics. The odds that another rocket will kill someone in exactly the same spot have got to be pretty low.

The shrapnel came in here It left here

The other thing about this place is well illustrated by the map I referred to a few weeks back: <http://www.cbc.ca/news/interactives/gmaps/afghanistan/>.

Canadian deaths have been clustered even more closely around FOB Leopard than around FOB Lynx. Not surprisingly, this is the site of one of the more moving memorials to our fallen that you will find in Afghanistan. The cross at the memorial is inscribed simply: "We Remember—*Nous Nous Souvenons.*"

"We Remember—Nous Nous Souvenons"

Quite a dramatic title, eh? Were you thinking that I was going to talk about Taliban infiltration of the ANA and ANP? Hoping for tales of cloak-and-dagger, watching men for tell-tale signs of treachery, capturing spies and then "making them talk"?

Sorry to disappoint you.

The enemy I refer to is the cause of more medical downtime in this war than any other single cause: infectious diseases.

It must be said that things have improved quite a bit in the last hundred years. During sailing trips I have led around the Caribbean, I have delved into the medical aspects of the various armies that sought to establish empires in the region. The situation for troops coming to the tropics from Europe was dismal. It was not unusual for troops stationed on these idyllic islands to experience *mortality* rates of 50 per cent—and this was when there was no war going on. Dysentery, typhus, yellow fever and, above all, malaria, decimated the ranks.

A little historical aside. Even people in the medical field in Canada have difficulty appreciating the impact of malaria on human health. It infects 300 million people a year and kills approximately 3 million of them. In his book *The Fourth Horseman*, Andrew Nikiforuk makes a convincing case that, until fairly recently, malaria had killed half of all the human beings who had ever died. Ever.

It was Dr. Ronald Ross, a British doctor working in India in 1897, who proved that malaria was transmitted by anopheline mosquitoes. Dr. Ross was something of a renaissance man. The day after making his discovery (for which he would be awarded the 1902 Nobel Prize for Medicine) he wrote a poem. It was called:

> **IN EXILE, REPLY—WHAT AILS THE SOLITUDE**
> This day relenting God hath placed within my hand
> A wondrous thing; and God be praised. At His command
> Seeking His secret deeds with tears and toiling breath
> I find thy cunning seeds, O million-murdering Death.
> I know this little thing a myriad men will save.
> O Death, where is thy sting, thy victory, O Grave!

Dr. Ross may have been sleep-deprived when he came up with the title, but he was definitely right about saving "a myriad men." He could have called it "*billion*-murdering death"—it would have been more accurate, but it would not have had that nice alliteration.

As with all things, the benefits of Dr. Ross's discovery did not fall evenly on the world's population. The armies of the developed world now rarely lose soldiers to the scourges of the nineteenth century. The situation for the citizens of the tropics, on the other hand, remains depressingly similar. During the Nicaraguan war, trauma of all types, war-related or not, never broke into the top five causes of mortality in that country. These five were all infectious diseases, with childhood dysentery (diarrhea caused by bad water) in first place. Tuberculosis was so prevalent that it rated a category all by itself (fifth), even though "respiratory infections" also rated a spot (second).

Things are far better for the Canadian Forces of 2007 than for virtually any army that has gone into the field before us. Nonetheless, our troops in the combat area are in an environment where the transmission of various pathogens is facilitated. We live fairly close together. We are often dirty, tired and under stress. Cleanliness is difficult to maintain.

So it was not entirely surprising that I arrived here to find the camp on the verge of an outbreak of gastroenteritis (vomiting and diarrhea). There had been seven cases in three days, and six more were diagnosed in my first two days here.

There were two obvious problems. A quick tour of the latrines showed that two-thirds of them did not have hand sanitizer. I had noticed a lot of people coming out of the latrines without washing their hands. Not their fault, if the army did not give them the wherewithal to do so. Easy fix: I went to the supply shacks, got a couple of cases of sanitizer and put one bottle in each latrine.

The next problem was trickier. There was a hand-washing station near the mess tent (the place the troops eat), but it was far from the entrance—fewer than a quarter of the soldiers were using it. The soap dispensers were broken. Worst of all, there were no paper towels. The troops who did wash their hands would dry them on their combat uniforms, effectively negating the good they had done.

This took a bit more effort. Much to the amusement of the rest of the medical staff, I got a shovel and rake and flattened out a platform right beside the entrance to the food-serving line. I then dragged the hand-washing stations over. I drilled small holes in the tops of empty water bottles and put some hand soap in them. Then I located a massive supply of paper towels (which had apparently been there for months) and had some crude dispensers made for them.

Now it was time to change some long-standing behaviour patterns. I spent forty-eight hours guarding the mess hall. No one got by me without washing their hands. As you can imagine, I took a fair amount of guff from the troops, but after two days I could stand back and watch the effects: troops lining up to wash their hands!

Addendum, December 29, 2007: We are now five days gastro-free! This may be my single greatest contribution to the war effort.

DECEMBER 23 | The Leopards Go Hunting

My first combat operation with the tanks. Once again we were teamed up with the Brits. The details of this operation are not relevant to the main point I want to make, so I will describe it only briefly. Our tanks took up a position north of here to give fire support to the British, who swept through the area north of the tanks in an east-west direction, clearing suspected compounds. Canadian infantry was positioned even farther north and off to one side to cut off the most likely escape routes.

What is important about this Op is not the way it was conducted but rather the result, which I think is even more noteworthy than the outcomes of the two operations I described earlier. And that result was . . . nothing. We spent the entire day clearing a large swath of Taliban territory, and not a single shot was fired. We found some weapons caches, which is always nice, but it might as well have been a peacetime exercise against an imaginary enemy force.

Armoured vehicles on the move

It is clear that the Taliban have a fairly effective early warning system. They have people watching the FOBs, and it is not possible to conceal the departure of a detachment of tanks and other armoured vehicles. What is very interesting is what they chose to do with that information: they ran. After the two shit-kickings we administered to them earlier this month, they have ceded the ground to us. And remember, this is their home base. Now try to reconcile the Taliban in their home turf of the Panjwayi running and hiding from a relatively small number of Canadians and Brits with the Senlis Council prediction that they will take Kabul in 2008. That's two weeks from now.

Addendum, June 1, 2009: It is now eighteen months past the time the Senlis Council predicted the Taliban would take Kabul. They are still raising a lot of ruckus, but they are no closer to taking the capital now than they were a year and a half ago. I should have called the Senlis Council and bet them a beer on that.

In some ways, this was the perfect time for me to come here. Had I left later, in May '08, as originally planned, my daughter, Michelle, might have taken it much harder. She has little sense of time right now. We talk on the phone every few days, and she seems happy with that. As for Christmas, she has no comprehension of what that is all about.

Being away from our families, there is not a whole lot of Christmas spirit at the FOB. Most of us put the whole holiday thing right out of our minds.

That having been said, we all thought it was damn decent of Peter MacKay, the minister of national defence, to come out here to spend the night with us, especially considering that the last time he visited a FOB (just last month) a rocket slammed right into the centre of the base. MacKay had to be thrown head-first into an armoured vehicle and spirited away. That could not have been fun for him, so it speaks well that he came back (and to "Rocket Central," to boot) to wish us Merry Christmas.

Damn! What's a life-long Liberal (nationally) and NDPer (provincially) to do? Get the celebrity picture, of course!

The celebrity pic

Addendum, December 20, 2008: I was so dismayed by the NDP and Liberal stance on Afghanistan that I actually voted Conservative in the last election. That's the first time I have done that in twenty-five years. I normally *hate* single-issue voters—I think they are bad for democracy—but this one was just too important to me. I was therefore very pleased when my current M.P., Glenn Thibeault, an NDPer, came to hear me speak and then asked me out to lunch. I took the opportunity to ask him how it was possible that our mission in Afghanistan was not supported by the party of feminism and education. He agreed that I had made some valid points and said he would try to get me in to speak to the NDP caucus. That should be interesting (if it ever occurs).

DECEMBER 25 | Thoughts of Home

Christmas Day. Michelle may not have a clue what all the adults are excited about, but I certainly do, and it is hard to be away from my daughter at this time. This brings us to the point of this diary. I have come to understand that my mother, who first suggested I keep a journal, was right (as mothers always are). I am writing this diary for my daughter. I hope that she reads it one day to better understand her dad. I hope the world is a better place when she does. I hope my efforts will have contributed to that.

That being the case, let me begin today's entry with an anecdote about my daughter.

My wife likes to sleep in, whereas I am an early riser. Before I left, I would often take care of Michelle by myself for an hour or two in the mornings. We had a routine. She would wake up and start calling *"Allo."* I would go into her room, and she would say *"En haut"* (French for "Up," which meant she wanted to be picked up). I would take her in my arms and ask her what she wanted. She would point towards the door and say *"La bas"* ("Over there"). Once we were out of her room, she would point down the stairs and say *"En bas"* ("Down"). I would carry her down the half-flight to my office.

Michelle with Dad: *"Encore!"*

It was anybody's guess what she would want to do next. She usually wanted to play in the living room or in my office. ("What is it about this room Daddy finds so interesting? He sure spends a lot of time here.") So we would hang out for a while and eventually have some cereal together.

In the two weeks before I deployed, one of her favourite games during these hours was for us to have our picture taken. I would hold the camera at arm's length and snap the shot. Then I would show it to her, and she would say: "Papa. Michelle. Encore!" We could keep doing this for twenty minutes. Gotta love digital!

When I got to Afghanistan, many of those pictures were still on my camera—a nice little bonus of mementoes I had not expected.

Back to Afghanistan. The crew commander, Gino, plays the guitar very well. He plays soft, almost mournful classical tunes. I realize this is right out of the movies, but when he started to play I couldn't help but stop what I was doing and just listen to the music . . . and think of my family. Two soldiers, in a bunker halfway around the world . . . wishing we were home.

Wishing we were home

Michelle with Mom

Christmas day was almost over when Gino decided to play a tune by Zachary Richard, an Acadian artist.* The song is "Jean Batailleur" ("Jean the Fighter"). I first heard it on an album my wife, Claude, bought for me years ago. It is a haunting song that speaks of terrible loss and terrifying loneliness, of hard lives lived *"au bout du monde"* ("at the ends of the earth"), of a fighter who finds himself without a family.

I have always found the melody incredibly powerful and almost unbearably sad. Before Gino was done singing the first verse, there were tears streaming down my cheeks.

I miss my wife and daughter very much.

DECEMBER 26 | No Connection

In the November 15 entry, I described how we were issued with cards that enabled us to call home for a certain number of minutes each week. This number was far too low for my family's needs. Claude and Michelle both needed to talk to me a great deal for the first several weeks. It has only been recently that Claude has gotten into the "rhythm" (if you can call it that) of the war. She now is fairly relaxed and does not need to talk to me as much as she did during those first weeks.

Until now, however, I needed to get more access to the phone lines than I was entitled to. There is no way to buy more time—I would have gladly done so—so I bartered for it with other soldiers who, for whatever reason, had more time than they needed. There are a number of troopers who have a *lot* of extra minutes. A couple of them, in fact, have used almost none of the time allotted to them—their minutes have been accumulating on their cards since their tour began. One of these two is an e-mail fanatic, the kind of guy who will have an entire conversation with his girlfriend by text message rather than talking to her. I'm not concerned about him—that's just one of those generational things,

---

* Zachary Richard was born in Louisiana and lives in Quebec. Like most French Canadians, I consider him to be one of us.

like the boys playing *Call of Duty*. But the other one doesn't seem to have anyone to call. That worries me a fair bit. I accepted his minutes with gratitude, but I find myself checking on him more regularly than on the other troopers.

DECEMBER 27 | Two Solitudes? Not Here!

As I mentioned in the December 2 entry, the vast majority of Canadian soldiers currently deployed in Afghanistan are from Quebec. The medical team here, as it was at FOB Lynx, is made up entirely of Quebecers.

I am Franco-Ontarian, and about as hardcore a Canadian federalist as you can find. It has therefore come as a pleasant surprise to hear these Quebecers refer to themselves exclusively as Canadians. They talk about going home "to Canada," about what is going on back home "in Canada," about what "Canada" thinks of the mission. I have not heard a single separatist sentiment in all my time here. And my five-man bunker is home to two large Canadian flags. There are many others throughout the camp, at FOB Lynx and at KAF.

I suppose if I'd thought about it, I could have predicted that the kind of Quebecer who joins the Canadian Forces has a much higher likelihood of having federalist sentiments than his neighbour. But it is nevertheless quite pleasant to be with this many Quebecers who believe in our country.

DECEMBER 28 | A FOB-Specific Glossary

I must start by giving credit for the concept of this entry to an American soldier, Sergeant Albert Merrifield.

FOBBIT A large hairy creature with an odd odour made up of equal parts sweat and gunpowder. Lives in concrete shelters. Eats virtually anything. Can predict the point of impact of a rocket with more accuracy than radar.

Three FOBbits at play in their natural habitat

FOBIA Fear of going to a FOB.

FOBEARANCE Putting up with the body odour, snoring, farting, etc. of the other guys in the bunker with you, in the hopes that they will show FOBearance towards your revolting personal habits.

FOBODING The impending sense of doom that one feels when reporting for duty on a FOB.

FOBIDDEN Not allowed on a FOB. Alcohol and sex, for instance, are FOBidden at FOB Leopard.

DECEMBER 30 | Improvised Explosive Device

It was around 0900 when we heard the blast. Mike (the medic) and I were standing outside the bunker. We looked northeast and saw the mushroom cloud of smoke and dust a couple of kilometres from the

At the top of FOB Leopard mountain

base perimeter. There had clearly been a fairly large detonation, but there was no cause for concern yet. A number of benign explanations were voiced: engineers blowing something up, a rocket landing well short of its objective. We could see that it had been very close to the road. No one wanted to say "IED," though everyone was thinking about that possibility.

Two minutes later the answer came over the radio. IED. No big deal, only one casualty, category Charlie. This means "May need surgery within four hours." So everyone piled into the armoured ambulance and headed off, but not in a rush.

The reality proved to be far worse. As is often the case, the first report had been incomplete. There were five casualties, one of them severely wounded and unconscious. Nothing could be done for him. Corporal Jonathan Dion is Canada's seventh fatality for this rotation.

This is getting harder to take, but not for the obvious reason. This is not my first time around this particular block. I have been in war zones before, and my profession has made me intimately familiar with death. I almost certainly won't be coming back from this with post-traumatic stress disorder (PTSD) or anything more than minor flashbacks that will resolve quickly. I am not unduly affected by what I have seen and done.

What *is* starting to bother me, though, is something that is very difficult to avoid in a war zone: superstition. Since I have been in Afghanistan, I have been on-site for all the deaths and disabling injuries the Canadian Forces has suffered. The first episodes were at KAF, where I was just one M.D. on the team. The last two have happened to men on my FOB shortly after my arrival. There are several FOBs, so you see where I am going with this. It was statistically very unlikely that I would end up in the same place as all the casualties.

I care deeply about these men, and these coincidences are getting to me. I am beginning to feel like an albatross.

Addendum, January 1, 2008: Mike was the first to get to the dying soldier, and he did a superb job. Afterwards, however, he was quite affected by the experience. He had dealt with dead Canadians before, but never dying ones. He found this quite difficult, and we talked about it at length. Like any dedicated health professional, he questioned whether he could have done anything else that might have saved our comrade's life. We went over the case in detail, and I assured him that his performance had been flawless.

When our debriefing was finished, what do you think he did to unwind? You guessed it: he played one of these amazingly realistic video war games. This one was in a modern setting but the bullet hits, blood splatters and bodies crumpling to the ground were the same as in the one the FOB Lynx team played. This time, I recognized it for what it was: a young man blowing off steam in the same way he had since he hit puberty. It didn't look odd at all. It got his mind off what he had just gone through. That was good enough for me.

Things are still tough around here. Everyone is taking the death yesterday of Corporal Jonathan Dion hard. The end of the tour is in sight, and the troops had started to think that we might get out of here without losing anyone else. In the parlance of the war zone, we are all "short-timers," meaning there is not that much time left before we rotate back home.

It has been a lousy day for other reasons as well. This morning, the ANA found another IED on the road leading to the FOB, so we sent a team out to blow it up. These episodes always make you feel happy that we found the damn thing, but also nervous because it means the Taliban snuck another one in there.

There was more bad news this afternoon. The Taliban captured sixteen ANP officers yesterday. It is hard for me to understand why, in these situations, the ANP do not fight to the death. They must know what fate awaits them if they surrender. We have already found the bodies of ten of them—bearing the marks of barbaric torture—and the Taliban radio has announced that they are getting around to "judging" the other six. Don't get any illusions—these men are as good as dead. The Taliban do not let prisoners live. The only question is how badly they will be tortured before being executed.

With all that, no one was in much of a mood to do anything for New Year's. We all turned in for the night around 2200. Then something happened that I had not experienced before. I got a call at 2330 from the command post telling me to get the ambulance crew up and into the ambulance. Something was going down out in the dark, and they wanted some backup from the QRF, the quick reaction force. We would be sending tanks, infantry and a medical team. I would stay at the unit medical station (UMS).

I realize they train for this, but I found the crew's reaction remarkable. From a deep sleep, they had their gear on and the ambulance fully loaded in a few minutes. In the dark. In the cold. They then hung around the UMS until the rest of the QRF got itself together. I wished them a happy New Year as they drove into the night.

Returning from a mission

I had seen these guys go out on similar watch-and-wait missions several times before. But there was something about this particular departure.

I think it was a combination of things: our recent loss, the time of year, the time of night, the fact that the mission was unclear and the way I am becoming more and more a part of the team here. For these and probably other reasons I can't quite express yet, I found myself more acutely worried for my friends' safety on this mission than I had ever been before. It was a physically uncomfortable feeling.

They came back around dawn. Some bad guys ended up dead, and that's great—but I was far happier about the fact that our people, and especially my medical buddies, had made it back without a scratch.

JANUARY 2, 2008 | ARV

There is one armoured vehicle I have not described yet: the armoured recovery vehicle, or ARV. It is at the centre of one of the many heart-warming stories that you will never hear in Canada.

The ARV is a bit bigger and a whole lot more powerful than a tank. It performs a myriad of functions: bulldozing, towing, digging, welding, mobile repair shop, you name it—it's a mobile heavy-vehicle repair shop plus earth mover plus heavy transporter. For a guy like me who has zero experience with heavy machinery, it is hard to comprehend what the ARV can do: it can pick up a seventy-ton tank and lift it out of a ditch.

For some reason (no one I have talked to can explain why), the ARV does not have a cool name like Husky, Bison or Leopard. It's just an "ARV," which sounds more like an involuntary bodily function than a war machine. To make things even more unfair, it has an almost-identical twin called a Badger. Instead of having a crane, the Badger has a digging bucket on the end of its boom. This vehicle is run by the engineers and is sometimes called an AEV (armoured engineer vehicle).

Be that as it may, the lack of a cool name in no way detracts from the fact that ARV crews are probably the least-recognized heroes of this war. I have heard countless stories from infantry and tank crews about ARV people repairing vehicles under direct enemy fire. This has to be one of the most difficult things to do in combat. The infantryman is actively shooting back. The medic rushes out, does the absolute minimum to

ARV, side view

keep the casualty alive, then drags his patient back to safety. These guys get their wrenches and pliers out and start trying to get a tank track back on while bullets and RPG rounds are whizzing by their heads. And they continue to do so even when they lose one of their own. One of the ARVs here is called "Calgary" in honour of the hometown of ARV crewman Corporal Nathan Hornburg, killed in action on September 24, 2007, while repairing a tank under fire. Unbelievable!

I could recount any one of these stories in detail, but I would not do justice to the courage of these soldiers. Combat defies the descriptive skills of authors far abler than I am. Let's just say that these guys all deserve a lot more recognition than they get and leave it at that. The story I want to tell you shows a completely different side to their work and to our efforts here.

The village near FOB Leopard has grown considerably in the last twenty-five years. In doing so, it has grown right around a Russian tank that had been knocked out and abandoned in the 1980s. Anything that could be removed for scrap had been, but that still left more than thirty tons of immovable metal stuck in the middle of one of the neighbourhoods.

Badger AEV breaking something

I am not sure what finally prompted the request, but one of the participants at a recent *shura* asked Major Robichaud (see the December 4 entry) if it would be possible for us to remove the tank carcass. The villagers wanted to expand some buildings, and there was no more room to do so. Major Robichaud arranged for the ARV to be sent in when it was convenient for the villagers.

When the sergeant in charge of the ARV got on site, he took a look at the layout and found that there was no way he could get the ARV-plus-tank combo out through the narrow streets. He informed the locals of this, but they surprised him by answering, "So long as you don't touch this wall or that wall, you can knock that other wall down."

I should mention that ARV crews are inordinately happy when they get to break something. Maybe they have gotten frustrated with fixing things all the time while the rest of the soldiers get to blow things up. For whatever reason, this was music to their ears. They unfortunately forgot their cameras, so you will have to use your imagination to picture what happened next.

The ARV manoeuvred right up to the tank. To do so, the crew had to rotate the ARV ninety degrees. It is possible to do this with tracked vehicles, by having one track go forward while the other one is in reverse, but it is a lot trickier than that brief description might lead you to believe. This was made even harder by the fact that they only had a few inches clearance on either side. Somehow, they did it.

And now comes the amazing part. Partly winching, partly towing, they basically rammed thirty tons of Soviet garbage through a thick mud-brick wall and clean out of town! The tank was immediately swarmed by children. Instant jungle gym!

So it was already a good day, and it ended on an even happier note. Two Taliban trying to rig a VBIED, a vehicle-borne IED, near our FOB blew themselves up. We heard the explosion in the middle of the night and when we went to check out the source of the noise we found what was left of their bodies—not much. That happens from time to time and is a source of satisfaction, relief and hilarity.

As I mentioned in my December 10 entry, I dragged a portable ultrasound unit all the way out here from Canada. What I did not describe was the effort required to do so. Although it is the size of a laptop, the unit is not something you can stuff in your back pocket. It had to be carefully packed and delicately transported, sometimes in fairly arduous conditions.

Until today, the unit had served as my security blanket. I am so used to working with ultrasound that I no longer feel comfortable practising without it. Even though I had not found any injuries or diseases with it, I felt reassured to have it here. As well, it had been good fun to teach the medics the rudiments of bedside ultrasound.

And then, today, all of the trouble I went through to bring the system here was made worthwhile. You can probably figure out where this story is going. Let's draw things out with some background.

Something I had not mentioned earlier is that when the ANA troops go on the road, they do so in completely unarmoured pickup trucks. When they hit IEDs, their casualties are much more severe and numerous than those we suffer in similar incidents in LAVs. And yet, they keep going out, day after day. You will no doubt recall my description of the emotions one goes through while riding in an armoured vehicle down the roads of Zhari/Panjwayi (see the December 18 entry). Now try to think of how it would feel going down those roads in a pickup.

This is another story that does not make it into the media back home. The ANA troops are incredibly brave. In speaking to members of the OMLT teams (the ANA's "mentors"—see the December 11 entry), you will hear constant admiration of the willingness of their ANA comrades to go forward under fire.

ANA pickup hit by IED

It must also be said that the ANA soldiers I have met have a deep hatred of the Taliban. No matter how well informed I am when I write about fighting the Taliban because they were horrible abusers of human rights, I will always be speaking in abstract terms. These men have lived it. They often tell me stories of abuses they suffered at the hands of the Taliban, sometimes relating the murder of entire families.

Martin Luther King once said, "An eye for an eye leaves everybody blind." I agree with him—but when you hear about some of the atrocities these men experienced, it is hard to begrudge them a little payback.

So on to today's story. The ANA and the OMLT, the operational mentoring and liaison team, had been chasing some Taliban when one of the ANA pickups rolled over, ejecting the soldiers riding in the back. One of them came in complaining of left hip pain. His airway was clear. He had good air entry in both lungs. His blood pressure and pulse were entirely normal. He had no abrasions or contusions, and his abdomen was soft, with only minimal tenderness in the left lower quadrant. His pelvis was stable. He had no neurological findings. All his limbs had full range of motion. At this point, almost without thinking about it, I reached for my bedside ultrasound machine. For me, the ultrasound examination of the chest and abdomen of a trauma patient has become an extension of my physical exam, a pro forma thing I do on everyone, even very low-risk patients such as this one. But.

In spite of that benign presentation . . . there it was!

In the right upper quadrant (around the liver)!

Internal bleeding!

What?

I had been thinking I would observe this guy for an hour or two, give him some analgesics and send him home. The patient had been thinking the same—he was quite surprised when I told him he was going to KAF for possible surgery. In less than an hour we had him in a medevac helicopter, a Blackhawk.

This story goes on to have a classic bedside ultrasound finish. When the patient arrived at KAF, he was starting to show signs of hemodynamic instability (he was going into shock from his internal blood loss),

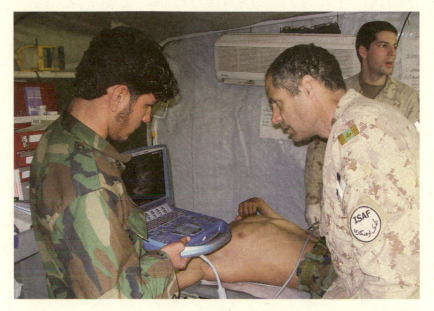

What? (I look a little stunned, don't I?)

so he went straight to the operating room. Liver and spleen lacerations were repaired, and a small hole in the bowel was oversewn. He will do very well, thanks to ultrasound-assisted early detection of his lesion and prompt referral to a surgical facility.

YES!

Addendum, April 19, 2009: The above case, and others like it that you will read about in later entries, had quite an impact in the CF Health Services. All the M.D.s and PAs who deployed to Afghanistan on TF 1-09 (which left Canada early this month) took an EDE course I taught in Montreal last December, and last month I went to CFB Val Cartier to certify three of them as instructors. I was also able to get an ultrasound company to donate three portable machines for use by my trainees on the FOBs. This morning I received an e-mail from one of them, describing how he was using the ultrasound machine almost daily.

This will be the first Roto where a significant number of the M.D.s and PAs will have had rigorous ultrasound training. It will be interesting to see how the use of ultrasound in Canadian military medicine evolves.

JANUARY 4 | The Weather (REALLY Not Much Going On)

In the November 23 entry, where I described my arrival at FOB Lynx, I predicted the imminent arrival of the rainy season and the transformation of the dust of the FOB into "a sea of mud." It turns out that this was a misconception, one that was relayed to me by folks who had been at KAF on previous tours. Here in the Panjwayi, so close to the Registan Desert, the "rainy season" means two days of rain in December and five in January. We had one yesterday. It was just long enough to tamp down all the dust. The FOB is no longer blanketed with a cloud of grey when helicopters land. Not a bad deal.

On the other hand, the temperature has gone down considerably. It is now advisable to time your bowel movements for midday, when the cold plastic latrine seats are barely tolerable.

JANUARY 6 | The Weather, Again (NOTHING Going On)

It has been raining for three days now. It looks like all of the above-mentioned five days of rain for January are going to come one after the other.

We had an out-and-out storm yesterday. There used to be a row of latrines across the valley from the unit medical station, the UMS. The photo shows where they were this morning. Have you seen the movie *Field of Dreams?* Would "Field of Outhouses" do as well?

Field of outhouses

I wrote yesterday's entry in the late afternoon. I wish I could write about boring stuff today.

For the past four days, we have been running a "sweep and clear" operation similar to the one described in the December 23 entry ("The Leopards Go Hunting"). We have been clearing terrain in the western parts of Zhari and Panjwayi districts and setting up new outposts. These will restrict Taliban movements even more. This is the deepest part of their home turf. Once we push them out of here, there is only the desert.

Things had been going very well. Virtually no enemy contact, as the Taliban seem to have lost the will, or the ability, to fight back. Some insurgents were captured, along with some weapons. It looked like the new outposts would be completed ahead of schedule.

Last night, around 1830, I got a call in the UMS that one of our vehicles had rolled over. The incident had occurred about ten kilometres from our FOB. Gino, the crew commander, and I reported to the command post (CP) to see what we could do to help. We were told that there was one fatality and one category Alpha (top priority). Attempts were being made to extricate the victims, after which they would be medevaced to KAF by helicopter directly from the crash site, given the seriousness of the Alpha casualty. There was no need for us to go out.

Gino and I decided to stay at the CP and listen to the radio traffic, to see how things evolved. We had both seen multiple examples of situations changing as more information came in. We ended up staying there over two hours.

Listening to the radio, it was obvious that the accident scene was right out of Dante's ninth circle of hell.

It was dark, very dark. The sky was completely clouded over. The nearest electrical light would have been kilometres away. Because of the presence of the enemy in the area, the men struggling to save their comrades would have been working only with the faint illumination of red "tactical" lights.

It was raining. It had been, for three days. The dust of the Panjwayi had turned to sticky, gritty mud.

It was cold. The temperature has been below freezing at night lately.

The vehicle, a LAV, was upside down in a muck-filled gully some ten metres deep. The men were trapped underneath it.

After two hours of listening to descriptions of people working as hard as they could in horrendous conditions, we heard the message, "We have gotten the first body out." The grammar was ominous. I immediately turned to Gino and said, quietly, so no one could hear: "First body? That means there is a second body. I don't think we have an Alpha on our hands." Tragically, I was right. A few minutes later the message came into the CP that our second comrade was dead as well. Both of the dead had been in the LAV's turret when the vehicle rolled. Two other soldiers who had been in the crew compartment were unhurt.

As we all do after these events, I logged on to the Web as soon as the news was officially released to see how the event was being reported. I was quite dismayed by what I saw.

This accident occurred because our troops and our vehicles are operating under combat conditions. They are good drivers, and the vehicles are sound. In combat, our troops have to accept a higher level of risk in all of their activities.

They drive down roads that are barely worthy of the name, dirt tracks with no signs to show them turns or road edges or hills. They drive down inclines that are at the very limits of their vehicles' tolerance. They drive at night with the lights off, looking through night-vision scopes that restrict their field of view and rob them of their depth perception. They ride with their hatches open, standing up in the turret. This exposes them to enemy fire and to the risk of being thrown or crushed if the vehicle rolls over. They do it anyway so that they can be more aware of the battlefield, so they can react more quickly to an enemy contact. And they drive as fast as they can under the existing conditions.

They do all these things because that's the only way they can do their job. That job is the hardest one in the world: to kill someone who is trying to kill them. They need every edge they can get. The only way to get that edge is to work at the limits of machine and human tolerance. They train for that, and almost always it works to their advantage.

This is why it disappointed me to see these deaths described as "not combat-related." Rather, the event has been reported as "an unfortunate accident." Bull-fucking-shit. If these men had not been engaged in combat operations they would not have been driving down a road that was marginal (at best), in a storm, at night, with their bodies exposed to the elements. They drove the way they did in the place they did to do their duty. What they were doing took tremendous courage and fortitude. They were fully cognizant of the risks they faced, and they went forward anyway.

These men were killed in action, advancing against the enemy.

We should honour these men for going down that road the way they did, and make sure people understand why they did it. To treat this as a "motor vehicle accident" denigrates what they were doing.

These men were killed in action, fighting the Taliban.

JANUARY 8 | Remembrance and Reaction

We held a service this morning for Warrant Officer Hani Massouh and Corporal Éric Labbé, who were killed in action on January 6. We gathered at the base of the memorial I described in the December 19 entry. The event looked just like the one in the picture (next page), which is of the memorial held for Corporal Nathan Hornburg last September. The photo shows the FOB Leopard memorial. The cross shown in my December 21 entry is visible on the right. The stones at the base of the maple leaf display the names of all the Canadian soldiers killed in the area. This is the only way I can show you what it looked like. Since I was participating in today's ceremony, I did not want to take any pictures.

The most senior officer from the Van Doos currently at the FOB was one of the platoon commanders, a young lieutenant. It fell to him to run the service. This officer is highly respected by his men for being a true warrior, absolutely fearless under fire. But you could tell that he was one of those people who is uncomfortable speaking in public (the most common phobia). He honoured our comrades, to be sure, but with

FOB Leopard memorial for Corporal Nathan Hornburg

words that were efficient and economical, rather than passionate and inspiring.

The reaction of my comrades is not exactly what I would have expected. It is quite different from the way I react. I am deeply saddened by our losses, but at no point do I lose control of my emotions. I am subdued for a couple of days afterwards as I deal with my grief.

The younger soldiers, in contrast, reacted very emotionally to the news of these latest deaths. The next morning, however, they were right back to joking and horsing around and seemed relatively unaffected. No discussion of the deaths took place, no venting occurred. Judging from past experience, I know some of them will come to me later to discuss their sleep issues. I am certain that others will seek out friends or trusted superiors to talk. I'm not yet sure whether this delayed processing of their grief has positive or negative implications.

Perhaps these younger soldiers have been better prepared for war than their forebears. Before deploying to Afghanistan, each Roto trains together for more than a year. The training is intense and realistic. They arrive here knowing, without a doubt, that some of them will not be going home alive. Maybe that's why they roll with that punch better than I thought they would.

There is also the possibility that it will hit them a lot harder than they expect when they get back. One of them said to me this morning that Remembrance Day was going to be very different for him this year. He had been in the army for seven years and had participated in many Remembrance Day parades. He had been polite to the veterans, but he had seen the tasks as boring and a nuisance. Now, he said, he would be remembering his friends, and it would have much more meaning for him. When I pointed out to him that he would be a veteran himself next November 11, he reacted with surprise: "Oh yeah! That's right!" I guess he had not fully realized that until I told him.

For me, Remembrance Day has always been very emotional. I feel a tremendous debt of gratitude towards our veterans and a tremendous sadness for our losses. As I mentioned earlier, I had gone to Normandy for the sixtieth anniversary of D-Day. I realized that this was one of the last chances we would have to see a large group of veterans all together. My goal was to shake hands with as many of them as possible and to say "Thank you for getting out of that boat." That was all I wanted to say, but I never managed it. In an entire week with over one hundred hand-shakes, I never got all the words out. I would choke up halfway through.

I expect things will be even more difficult next November. Warrant Officer Massouh sat across from me during briefings at the FOB Leopard command post. I had treated Corporal Labbé for a minor ailment. These will never be just names to me.

JANUARY 9 | Media Relations, Part One

Let me begin with a story from an earlier war. When I got to Nicaragua in June 1987, the Contra war was raging. I spent the next year visiting the health posts of the northern war zone teaching a "culturally appropriate" advanced trauma life support course. On Christmas Day, 1987, I was working at the main hospital in my area, located in a town called Matagalpa. I was replacing one of the hospital staff, to allow him to have Christmas with his family.

At approximately 2100, the first Canadian to die in that conflict was brought to my hospital. She was a member of an aid organization that was working in the country. She had been hit by shrapnel from a hand grenade and had bled to death before she arrived. She was beyond saving, so I attended to the evening's other casualty, a Nicaraguan soldier. After I had stabilized him, I went to find the other members of the dead Canadian's group to inform them of their colleague's death. They were staying at a farm some twenty kilometres out of town.

By the time I was finished breaking the bad news, it was around 0100. The only people who knew there was a dead Canadian in Nicaragua were her Canadian colleagues, the hospital staff and a few military officers. None of the Canadians had any access to communications equipment. Unless you worked in the developing world twenty years ago, it might be difficult to understand how cut off these people were, so let me emphasize it. There was no way they could talk to anyone outside their farm. None.

There was some phone equipment in Matagalpa, but it was notoriously unreliable. Even in that town, a provincial capital, I once had to call every single day for two weeks before I was able to get a line to Canada. I went to bed that night thinking I would have time to deal with the situation in the morning.

When I woke up, I went back to the farm where the Canadians were staying and brought their leader back to town to identify the body and start to track down the family. Thinking to get ahead of the curve, I called the CBC stringer in Managua, the national capital. I knew him fairly well, and I told him what had happened. My reasoning was that he might find out about the death some other way, and I wanted to make it clear to him that the family did not know yet. I begged him for the chance to contact the family before he released the information. He readily agreed, but what he said next stunned me: "You'd better hurry up. It's already on the news wires."

I couldn't believe what he was saying! It was Boxing Day. It was 1000, thirteen hours after the death had occurred in an end-of-the-road, developing-world village. Most of those hours had been night-time. And yet teletype machines were already clattering away all over the world announcing the death of this Canadian.

I worked as hard as I could for the next five hours, but to no avail. I managed to reach the dead woman's parents and siblings, but none of them knew where her husband was. He was visiting friends they did not know, and no one had cell phones back then.

The husband heard the news of his wife's death on the radio at 1500.

The Canadian Forces is determined not to let that happen to any of our military families. When we suffer combat deaths or serious inju-ries, the CF ensures that the fact that a Canadian has been killed or badly wounded is kept confidential until the family has been notified. All communications with the outside world are "locked down." The Internet shack is locked, the phones are disconnected and only essen-tial communications are allowed. As far as I know, these efforts have always been successful. Not only does this prevent disasters like the one I have just described, but it also protects all the other families. If my wife or my parents hear of a Canadian death on the radio or TV, they can be sure that it does *not* refer to me.

This process of keeping the information confidential begins on the battlefield. The only identification that gets read over the radio is the dog tag number of the dead man. That was all Gino and I had heard when we were in the command post. I noticed Gino writing the numbers down, but I did not realize why. I soon learned that was all he needed.

When we returned to the bunker to give the bad news, I understood what he had done. Other medics, attached to the various combat units, had gathered in our bunker. Everybody knows the "number only" rou-tine. Close friends will learn each other's numbers so that they will know whether their buddies are alive or dead. When Gino and I walked in, we were met by faces pleading with us not to say those particular numbers. One medic was hyperventilating; another was like a stone statue. All of them were looking at us with varying degrees of distress. Some of them had been crying.

When Gino read the numbers out, there was silence . . . then a long, slow, collective exhalation. No one had lost a close friend.

This time.

JANUARY 10 | Media Relations, Part Two

I mentioned that the media pay a lot of attention to us whenever a Canadian is killed. I am conflicted about this. On the one hand, I want the sacrifice of our fallen to be recognized. On the other, I wish they would do a better job of placing our losses in context. For the media to place so much emphasis on the death and not on the conflict in which it occurred does a real disservice to the Canadian population. This is a war we're involved in. There are going to be casualties. They should be honoured, but they should not be the whole story.

I am most bothered by the way the media make a point of keeping a running total of our deaths but not of our successes. Virtually every article about a Canadian being killed here includes the sentence: "That makes it seventy-six Canadians killed in Afghanistan since the mission began" or something along those lines. Why do we almost never hear the statistic that makes those deaths worthwhile: under the Taliban, there were 600,000 students of all kinds (primary, secondary and university) in the country, 2 per cent of them female. Now, there are *six million, 20 per cent of them female.* And why are Taliban atrocities, which routinely kill dozens of civilians, never given more than a passing reference? If the media want to track numbers so much, why don't they keep a running tally of the number of children killed by Taliban bombs (which reaches into the hundreds every year)?

How about the most telling statistic of all? The one that proves, beyond the shadow of a doubt, that things are getting better here. As one of my wisest friends once told me, "It's easy to judge a government. Just go to the border and watch the flow."

During the Soviet occupation, there were around six million Afghan refugees outside the country, mostly in Pakistan and Iran. That was 50 per cent of *all* refugees worldwide. The Soviet occupation ran from 1979 to 1989. You may recall that the Ethiopian famine peaked in 1984, right in the middle of this period. Yet Afghans still dominated the refugee population of the planet. The reason for this is simple: even faced with famine, people will rarely stray far from their homes. Only war has the power to do that, particularly if it is waged with the brutality the Soviets inflicted on this country.

The mujahedeen victory in 1989 did little to change this situation. Various warlords fought each other for another five years in a vicious civil war, with a disregard for civilian lives that matched that of the Soviets. Kabul, the national capital, which had been relatively spared until that point, was bombarded into rubble. If there were not many more refugees produced during this period, it is because everyone who could leave had already done so. The civil war was so bad that those people who were still living in Afghanistan initially welcomed the Taliban. *Anything* seemed better than the anarchy that had reigned during the civil war. But the Taliban quickly showed their true colours, and the refugees stayed away.

Since the Coalition ousted the Taliban, the refugees have come flooding back—nearly all of them have returned. Think of the implications of that. Afghanistan is one of the world's poorest countries. Over the past five years over five million people, most of them destitute, have come back into the country after an absence of several years, if not decades. These people need housing, food, water, education for their children and medical care. You begin to understand the magnitude of the challenge facing us as we try to nation-build here. But regardless of the challenges, the people of Afghanistan have come back. This is their *home*.

Let me tell you the story of one of these returnees. You may recall that an Afghan interpreter was killed in the November 17 IED strike that killed two Canadians (see my November 18 entry). Pashto is quite difficult to learn, so such people are used extensively. The job is dangerous but the pay is commensurate with the risk, making this one of the higher-paying jobs available in the country. There is no shortage of volunteers.

I spent a couple of hours this evening talking to one such interpreter who works for the FOB Leopard OMLT (see my December 11 entry). He had left Afghanistan when the Taliban came to power and had built an excellent life for himself in Pakistan. He had become the manager of a large business, and he had a great life—money, a big house, a couple of servants, good schools for the kids. I asked him why he had come back, expecting to hear some idealistic stuff about rebuilding the country. Wrong! He said he loved it in Pakistan and he wanted to stay. He was making much more money there, he was safe and life was great. He would have been happy never to return to Afghanistan.

He came back because his entire extended family, having fled the Taliban, had all returned. So had every other Afghan he knew. His wife was terribly lonely, and his kids had no one to play with. Reluctantly, he left the job and the money and the house, and he followed. Tell me *that* doesn't have the "ring of truth"! Tell me why *that* doesn't get published in Canada.

This guy also told me that Afghans consider passing gas to be almost sacrilegious. One loud fart and you will be ostracized. As those who know me well will attest, this pretty much rules out a long-term involvement for me with any Afghan organization.

JANUARY 11 | Mike the Terp

There is another interpreter (or "terp," to use army slang) working here. He goes by the name of Mike, which is easier for the Canadians to remember than his real name. He has been helping me expand my knowledge of Pashto beyond the limited medical lexicon I learned before coming here.

Like a lot of Afghans, he goes by a single name. I would like to tell you that name, because he is probably the Afghan with whom I have had the most interaction. But I can't. It is important not to identify Afghans who are working with the Coalition by name, for their safety. Two contractors identified by a single name in a Toronto newspaper were murdered the day after their names were publicized in Canada. E-mail and the Internet have made the world a very small place.

It may interest you to know that Mike is a Hazara, one of the main ethnic groups in Afghanistan. He is from a city called Mazar-i-Sharif, in the north-central part of the country. This is Afghanistan's fourth-largest city.

You have probably heard of Srebrenica, the city in Bosnia where some eight thousand Muslim civilians (possibly more) were killed by Serbs in July 1995. This is the worst atrocity committed on the European continent since the end of World War Two. This was done despite the city having been declared a "safe zone" by the United Nations. There were four hundred armed Dutch peacekeepers in the city when the Serbs arrived. They could have called on other UN forces in Bosnia, including Canadians, to support them. Instead, the UN turned the city over to the Serbs.

In some ways, the failure of the West at Srebrenica is worse than our failure in Rwanda. We had sizable forces in and around Srebrenica, whereas in Rwanda the help General Roméo Dallaire needed was half a world away. We knew the Serbs had a record of atrocities going back several years, whereas the Hutu in Rwanda surprised us by turning genocidal in a matter of weeks. In spite of that, when the Serbs said "Boo!" we backed down without firing a shot.

Mazar-i-Sharif is the Afghan Srebrenica. In August 1998, the Taliban took the city and murdered eight thousand Hazara civilians, whom they considered infidels because they are Shia Muslims (the Taliban are almost all Sunni Muslims). The Taliban seemed to delight in killing their victims in ways designed to increase their suffering. This was the worst massacre of civilians in the thirty years that Afghanistan has been at war. Even the Soviets did not manage something like this during their brutal ten-year occupation.

You can read the definitive report on the massacre from Human Rights Watch at <http://www.hrw.org/reports98/afghan/Afrepor0 .htm>.

This is who we are fighting.

So that's it. My orders just came through. The PA I was replacing will return tomorrow, and I will go back to KAF. Indoor plumbing, restaurants, Tim Hortons, laundromats and so much less risk. I return to Canada in three weeks. It is now a near certainty that I am coming back from my tour without a scratch.

(On second thought, I wish I hadn't written that line—seems like I'm tempting fate.)

So why do I feel so melancholy?

When I called the Canadian Forces last April to volunteer for this posting, my motivation was to support the mission. That motivation, which I described fairly clearly in my first letter, had not changed when I got here. Something has definitely changed now. No, not changed. Something has been added.

The new element is what I feel for the soldiers I have lived with for the past two months. I wanted to support the mission, but the people I wanted to support were the people in combat: the troops who live on the FOBs and who go out day after day doing the bitterly hard work of war. I don't think I was fully aware of that when I got here. I certainly am now.

This feeling has been even more intense at FOB Leopard than it was at FOB Lynx. By the time I got here, I was into the routine of the FOBs and of the war. I integrated into the team very quickly and made real friends.

I spent this last day just hanging out with the medical team. I filmed Gino playing the guitar tune I had found most moving. I tried to convince Mike to apply to medical school. I talked with Frank about life, the universe and everything.

I am going to miss these men more than I can say. I will be watching their every move on the Internet and through my e-mail contacts. I feel like I am leaving them while they still need me, which is ludicrous. The PAS are all very competent and will look after them just fine.

All things considered, I could not have asked for a better assignment. I got to see more of Afghanistan than any other doctor deployed here. I met some great people and had a lot of good times. There were difficult moments, to be sure, but we got through them. Most importantly, I feel like I have made a contribution to the mission. I have been told that I hold the record as the doctor who has spent the most time in the combat area since the Canadian Forces came to Kandahar.

I'm sitting in the UMS writing this after one last long walk around the FOB, reflecting on the experience. I knew what I was getting into, so there were not many surprises.

There have been undeniable effects, however.

Getting dressed in the morning is not complete until my pistol is holstered and strapped to my leg. It will feel a little odd not to have it there anymore, but I don't think that will last more than a day or two. Nor do I think I will spend any time looking around for the rifle that was always beside my bed. I have not had to fire either of my weapons to defend myself, so I don't think I will be distressed by their absence. Like most Canadians, I see guns as being something which should be very difficult to acquire, kept under lock and key and used only in specific, controlled circumstances.

I now slip the heavy frag vest on with a single fluid movement. It feels like a second skin. I can't say the same for my helmet. Even after two months of regular use, it still feels awkward. Maybe that's because I think I look funny wearing it. Some people look tough wearing a helmet. I'm not one of those guys. Both these items gave me a lot of comfort, but that was directly related to the threat of rocket attacks. I would take them off as soon as I was under concrete. I will be happy to get rid of them.

I will certainly miss the pace of the FOB. I stated earlier that wars are 95 per cent boredom and 5 per cent terror. The 5 per cent was no fun at all, but after a decade and a half of intense medical work it was great to be able to spend time in quiet reflection. I haven't done a lot of that in my life.

What I will miss most of all is the feeling of being part of a group involved in something truly noble, something larger than ourselves. Modern life does not offer a lot of opportunities to feel like that. The significant exception is parenting. That will be my next challenge.

Last day with the FOB Leopard team

JANUARY 13 | Choppering Out

A lot of mixed emotions this morning.

Transportation-wise it was all good. I lucked out again and got a spot on a chopper. No road convoy for the trip back to KAF!

The team had a great sendoff for me. Normally, one is brought to the helicopter landing zone for these departures in a small ATV-like vehicle called a Gator. This morning, though, the crew insisted on taking me in the ambulance. As a special treat, Gino had me take his place in the crew commander's seat and they took me on a scenic tour all around the base for one more look at FOB Leopard. It was a wonderful moment. This was the nicest goodbye they could give me.

To my surprise, my ride was not a Blackhawk but rather the much smaller Lynx. This is a type of helicopter we rarely saw at the FOB. There was only room for three passengers. My two fellow travellers took their place on the port side. I was placed on the starboard side, beside the door gunner.

For the first few kilometres we flew just a few feet off the ground. This is called NOE flying, for "Nape of the Earth." This means that you fly as low as possible, hugging every contour of the ground as you go. This is quite challenging flying and is done to make us as difficult a target as possible for any Taliban who might have been lying in wait near the base. I am only aware of two Coalition helicopters that have been shot down by Taliban fire, but I appreciated the pilot's efforts.

After this, we climbed to several thousand feet and had a sedate flight until we got close to KAF. I could see the airfield, when the pilot suddenly initiated a steep dive and began a series of violent manoeuvres. I thought someone was shooting at us, but the door gunner was not training his weapon in any particular direction. Rather, he was sitting back beside me and smiling. I understood then that the pilots were just having a good time. I relaxed and enjoyed what has to be the best roller coaster ride you can imagine.

The vehicle the hospital had sent for me took me back to my shack, where I dumped my gear. I have a *lot* more space now than when I left! The reason for this relates to the emphasis today's army places on keeping the troops in the theatre of operations clean and sober (see my November 24 entry). While I was at the FOBs, one of my roommates was "re-pated" (repatriated—sent home in disgrace) for having snuck into a tent where the 0.5 per cent beer was being stored and having stolen a couple of extra cans. My remaining roommates, though sorry to see him go, had immediately turned his space into a storage area so we could all spread out a bit more.*

I then went to the hospital to report in. My commanding officer welcomed me back and told me to take the rest of the day off. I had not made it to the door when the "Curse of Ray" manifested itself yet again. Another one of our vehicles had hit an IED, and four casualties were coming in. What is it about my arrival, anywhere, that brings such bad luck to Canadian soldiers? Fortunately, the injuries were all minor.

---

* *Postscript, February 7, 2008:* As it turns out, I never got *any* of my two 0.5 percent beers a month. The army owes me eight beers.

After we had finished dealing with the casualties, the doctors gathered in our lounge area. The specialists (trauma surgery, orthopedic surgery, intensive care and anesthesiology) were in the process of changing over. Most of the specialists at KAF, whether military or civilian, spend only one or two months working at the Role 3 Hospital, so I met quite a few colleagues. The ones who were leaving had arrived after I left for FOB Lynx. The ones who were arriving had only been here for a few days.

The presence of the new specialists led to an interesting exchange. One of the civilians realized that I was a new face. When I explained that I had been "outside the wire" for two months, he asked me what that meant. As a civilian, he had little understanding of the war zone and was shocked at the level of danger my job had entailed. He then asked me how dangerous it was at the KAF base. I was still dusty and rumpled from my trip on the chopper, and I knew that KAF had not been hit by a rocket in weeks. So I was more than a little bit full of myself when I replied, "You are perfectly safe here."

Upon hearing this, a military surgeon who has been here since August became visibly irate and said, "That's not true. There have been rocket attacks, and there have been people who have tried to sneak bombs onto the base."

It was obvious that I had touched a nerve. I have probably touched a few more in prior diary entries where I expressed a certain amount of disdain for those who worked at KAF. There is a real FOB-KAF divide among the troops here, and it was probably inevitable that I would fall into it.

Hindsight shows me that this was inappropriate. The people who work at KAF are doing work that is essential to the mission. Most of them are more than willing to go to the combat area, but this is denied to them because they are irreplaceable if they are killed or wounded.

Although the KAF population is exposed to less risk than one assumes at a FOB, it is still a degree of risk far greater than they have to face in Canada. It was wrong of me to denigrate this. It also showed how short one's memory can be. On my third day at KAF last November, I found myself far from a shelter when the sirens warning of a rocket attack had sounded. I was very frightened when that happened.

Fortunately, in the interaction described above, I recognized my error and agreed with the doctor who had corrected me. I would now like to take this opportunity to apologize to readers of this diary who have served with distinction at KAF or who will do so in the future. I regret any offence my words may have caused you, and I salute your courage.

Addendum, February 6, 2008: I am out of Afghanistan, but I heard that a rocket landed on the KAF base yesterday. It hit so close to the quarters of the medical staff that the entire shack was violently shaken. There were no casualties, but obviously life at KAF is anything but "perfectly safe."

JANUARY 14 | Caring for a Fellow "FOBbit"

We had one more casualty today, again a victim of an IED. He was only roughed up and ended up needing little more than anti-inflammatory medication and a few days off.

I was not the primary doc looking after him, but I was asked by the treating physician to assist by performing a bedside ultrasound. I was setting up to do my exam when the casualty said "Hi, Doc!" in a voice that was a little tremulous but nonetheless quite cheerful. I looked down and recognized one of the men who had been with me at FOB Leopard.

It made for an emotionally interesting experience. On the one hand, I was quite happy to be helping to look after him. We talked about the FOB, and we laughed about the way I had forced everybody to wash their hands. I kept a steady patter going that I think he found quite comforting.

On the other hand, I found it more difficult to deal with him than with the casualties we had dealt with yesterday. This was "one of my guys," and it was harder to see him on the stretcher than it would have been had we not had that connection. If I feel this way after only two months, how much more intense must the feeling be for men who have trained and fought together for over a year?

A few days before I left FOB Leopard, a small reconnaissance unit from another FOB had joined us to participate in a particular mission. Since they were equipped with a vehicle I had not encountered before, I visited with them for part of an afternoon. They were gracious hosts, offering a guided tour of their vehicle as well as part of their supper.

When we heard this morning that another Canadian had been killed, we all went to the communications centre to get more information. As soon as we got there, I recognized the radio call sign of the unit that had received me so kindly a few days earlier. I had to walk out of the room quickly so that no one would see the tears in my eyes. It took a couple of minutes before I got my breath back.

About an hour later, I realized that the vehicle that had been hit had belonged to a sub-unit that had *not* visited FOB Leopard. I guess it is only human that my immediate reaction was one of relief.

Since my arrival, we have lost six men. It should not surprise you that the loss of the ones who were closer to me hurt more than the rest.

On D-Day, Canada lost 347 men. About one-sixth of these belonged to a single company of the Royal Winnipeg Rifles. Their assault craft drifted away from their assigned landing area and ended up depositing them directly in front of a German strongpoint. Some sixty men were killed within the first five minutes. This was roughly a third of the men in that company.

The remainder seized their objectives and proceeded inland.

These men had been together, training in England, for at least two years. Some had been together for far longer, having gone over in 1939, nearly five years before D-Day.

I have no idea how they kept on going, after losing so many friends. I am not at all sure I would have been able to.

JANUARY 16 | Farewell to a Friend

The ramp ceremony for Trooper Richard Renaud. My second one. A lot harder than the first.

If you have seen pictures of these ceremonies, you will have noticed that our soldiers are lined up five deep on either side. What you probably do not know is how we are divided.

By ancient tradition, the right side is considered the side of honour in any military formation. As our comrade's casket is carried towards the waiting aircraft, the soldiers on the right are members of the battle group, the combat units who do the actual fighting. The people on the left are members of the various support elements. As described in this diary's glossary, only a third of the 2,800 Canadians deployed in Afghanistan are combat troops.

As I was no longer a "FOB Doc" but rather a member of the Role 3 Hospital, I lined up on the left. I had wanted to line up in the rear, but a last-second change in our formation put me in the front rank.

I was quite close to the Hercules. Directly across from me were the members of the dead man's unit. I don't think they recognized me.

The image of those men, their faces wracked with sobs as they stood rigidly at attention saluting their comrade's casket, is one I will never forget.

JANUARY 19 | The FOB Connection

Two days ago, on January 17, we received four more casualties from yet another IED strike against one of our vehicles that had been performing mine-detection duties. Fortunately they were all minor contusions and abrasions.

We discharged two of them after an assessment and a few X-rays. The other two, including the one I was responsible for, were admitted overnight for pain management. They were both feeling much better yesterday morning and were discharged. The plan was to have them spend a week in KAF eating anti-inflammatories and doing physiotherapy, after which they would return to their units.

This evening, I was called back to the hospital. The patient I had admitted had returned and had been readmitted last night. He was in rough shape emotionally. He had had a number of nightmares and had been unable to sleep since his discharge. As he was being interviewed, he complained of a number of bizarre symptoms, such as total body itching, and he had a fainting spell. It was obvious that he was suffering from what we call CSR, combat stress reaction.

We have a psychiatrist here as well as a couple of mental health nurses, so you might be wondering why I was called. The reason will probably stay with me as the single proudest moment of my entire deployment. The patient had specifically requested to talk to me, stating: "Captain Wiss knows me. He was on the FOB with us. He knows what it's like out there."

More than any medals or accolades, those words from a front-line trooper will be the most significant reward I will receive for my service here.

I immediately went to his bedside, and we sat and talked for the better part of an hour. It was only when I saw him again that I remembered he had come to FOB Leopard towards the end of my time there and that I had photographed him and his vehicle. This is a classic example of how doctors sometimes "disconnect" from the patient to focus on their job.

I did all of the usual things you do in encounters of this kind, but there was one thing I said that seemed to help more than anything else. I told him that he had, in all likelihood, saved the life of several of his comrades. I joked that setting off the mine with the vehicle was perhaps not the best way to do his job, but in the final analysis he had accomplished his mission. I asked him whether anybody else had pointed that out to him. No one had, so I re-emphasized it. By exposing himself more than anyone else, he had protected his buddies. I am not sure I would have thought of that had I not served on the FOB.

As much as we all want to come back alive from this war, the feeling of brotherhood we have for each other on the battlefield makes us care more about our buddies than about ourselves. It took several minutes for what I had said to sink in. Ever so slowly, I watched as his fear turned to pride.

Addendum, January 20, 2008: The patient was doing much better the following morning. All of his bizarre body sensations had resolved, and he had not had any further nightmares. He was given his discharge from the hospital and will be returning to his unit after a few more days of rest.

A Brief Lecture on Combat Psychiatry

The reaction of human beings to the stress of combat is highly variable, and the concept of combat stress reaction (CSR) has only gained credence very recently. Until the last century, anyone who refused to fight was considered a traitor and executed. In the words of one French general, this was done *"pour encourager les autres"* (to encourage the others).

This began to change during World War One, when the term "shell shock" was used to describe men whose nerves had cracked under the prolonged bombardments typical of that conflict. For the first time, psychiatric treatments were attempted.

This was not immediately accepted by military establishments. Armies around the world continued to believe that individuals suffering from such conditions were weaklings, if not outright cowards.

We have come a long way since then. Today, a Canadian soldier with CSR can expect a sympathetic hearing from a competent mental health professional.

It is important to understand that it is best to treat CSRs as close to the front line as possible. Soldiers' feelings of self-worth are intimately bound up with their ability to withstand the rigours of combat. Although it may seem humane to allow soldiers suffering from CSR to remain in camp or even to go home, this is almost never the right treatment.

Soldiers who have to be removed from the theatre of operations because of CSR very frequently go on to develop serious, even life-threatening, mental illness. No matter what you tell them, in their hearts they will always believe that they let their buddies down, that they were not up to the task for which they had volunteered and for which they had been trained. This is absolutely devastating to a young soldier's self-esteem. It is not far from that point to depression and suicidal ideation.

This is why military doctors make it clear to CSR casualties that they are expected to return to duty as rapidly as possible—something civilians often have difficulty understanding.

JANUARY 20 | Interview

A few weeks before I returned to KAF, a CBC crew from the program *The Fifth Estate* arrived to produce a documentary about the Role 3 Hospital. It was my turn to be interviewed today.

Like any interview, whether with the media or for a job or for a spot in medical school, you can't help but walk away from it thinking of how you could have done better. It is clear, however, that writing this diary has forced me to think through my motivations and perceptions very thoroughly. If you ever see me in this interview (the documentary is scheduled for March 19, but who knows what they will choose to use in it) you will recognize certain turns of phrase that you have read in these pages. All in all, I think I did a good job of explaining myself and educating the interviewer about the purpose of the mission.

The only question I was not expecting, and that made me feel quite uncomfortable, was one about my feelings about the recent deaths we have suffered. The interviewer knew that I had served at the same FOB as these men, and she wanted to know how I was able to cope with the deaths of individuals I had known personally. I didn't have a ready answer for this and sputtered something about it being "really hard." How eloquent.

What I should have said was that I did not want to answer that question in front of a television audience. It's a question that only friends should ever ask. What I would tell you is that these deaths, though very difficult to bear, are an expected part of war and are justified by the goals of the mission.

Several hours after the interview, I bumped into the public affairs officer (PAO) who is escorting the documentary crew. He has quite a difficult job. He has to ensure that the crew does not record anything that could compromise operational security, while at the same time facilitating their work. As you can imagine, this leads to a certain tension between him and the CBC types!

While speaking to him, it became obvious that I had transgressed one of the basic rules for Canadian Forces officers being interviewed. I had been quite clear, even passionate, about the fact that I support the mission. That was inappropriate. The PAO told me that the army must, at all times, remain apolitical. This caught me completely by surprise. When he explained it further, I had to admit he had a point.

To express support for the mission is to express a political opinion. That is something soldiers must never do publicly. To express agreement with current government policy would open the CF to accusations of partisanship in the political process.

A soldier's greatest loyalty must be to the Canadian people. The government of the day is the expression of our people's will. Should the government change, our political leaders must still be entirely confident that the army remains at their service. Soldiers can choose to leave the army, at the end of their contract, if they disagree with the government's military policy. They can also refuse to follow an order that is immoral or illegal. Outside of those rare circumstances, they must display the utmost loyalty to their political masters, irrespective of whether they agree with their decisions or not. Anyone armed by the state in a democracy has to accept that.

I could see the validity of the argument, but I asked if it applied to me. I had not chosen to join the army as a career or even as a temporary job. On the contrary, I had specifically called the army last April to express my willingness to serve on a mission with which I was in complete agreement. I had been explicitly clear that I was enrolling only to serve in Afghanistan. The PAO agreed that this changed the situation somewhat.

Addendum, January 24, 2008: The PAO has been in contact with Ottawa, and it turns out that the people at National Defence Headquarters agree with me. The consensus of opinion is that my position during the interview was, at worst, appropriate. There is even a colonel (that's one rank below general) who thinks I did great. So, no firing squad for me!

Addendum, March 19, 2008: The episode has aired, and I am in it for at least two, maybe three, seconds. There is another spot where you see my right hand (doing a bedside ultrasound exam—how apt!) for a full second. And I have a speaking role! If you listen very carefully, you can hear me say "abdominal pain." Or at least, my mother says she heard that. I missed it completely.

I do believe I have . . . Star Quality!

JANUARY 21 | Night Shift

What's it like working a night shift at the KAF Role 3 Hospital? Well, it would be like working in a tiny hospital in northern Ontario that happens to be beside an airport where planes carrying up to ten people crash every few days. The odds are about four to one in favour of getting a whole lot of reading or paperwork done between 1830 and midnight and getting a good night's sleep between midnight and 0800. That also means the odds are one in four that the feces will hit the ventilation system in a big way.

Tonight, the odds have gone my way. It is now a bit past midnight and I have seen a grand total of two patients, one with a sore throat and one with back pain. At this time of night, combat activity in our area of operations is virtually zero. Chances are very good that no one will hit an IED or get shot until tomorrow.

I started off the shift like any good emerg doc: I bought coffee and doughnuts for everyone. This was facilitated by my brother Rob's Christmas present of Tim Hortons gift certificates. I received these only when I returned from the FOB, as the folks in the mailroom at KAF had "lost track" of me. I can't blame them. Not many soldiers have moved around Afghanistan as much and as quickly as I have.

Our "weather haven" structures are good at keeping the rain and snow off our heads, but the junction between the wall and the concrete floor leaks like a sieve whenever there is a heavy downpour. Fortunately, as a captain, I don't have to mop this stuff up every two hours—RHIP (rank has its privileges!).

Rank has its privileges

JANUARY 23 | Jelly Bean

His name was Jelly Bean.

I never knew his first name. It turns out no one did, not even the men who had been in the same vehicle with him for over eighteen months. It was the way he introduced himself, and everyone followed his lead. The way he told the story, he had been born prematurely and his head had been misshapen since birth. My bet is that he was teased mercilessly about it in childhood, so he decided to accept himself as he was and laugh in the face of those who would mock him.

He lived across the valley and up the hill from me at FOB Leopard. He was a combat engineer, tasked with mine detection.

When we got the call at the Role 3 Hospital, we were told he was an Alpha priority. We got ready, but then we were told he had died.

Five minutes later, we were told they were still trying to revive him. I went to the blood bank and told them to get all the type O blood they had ready to go. This is the blood type you can give to anybody. We then got two Level 1 Infusers set up (machines that can push a unit of blood into a patient in under a minute).

While we were getting that ready, they called us back to say that, despite their best efforts, his heart had stopped.

The other crew members of the armoured vehicle came in ten minutes after that. I was assigned to the crew commander. He seemed to only have suffered bruises, but I ordered a few X-rays to be sure. They were all negative.

When I was certain he was in no physical danger, I shooed everyone out of the trauma bay and closed the drapes. It was obvious that my patient was distraught and needed some time with as few people around him as possible.

The crew commander and I spent the next half hour talking. He was physically imposing, a strong man used to being able to control his emotions. What he has gone through today has wounded him as surely as shrapnel.

He blamed himself for not having detected the IED. He had been horrified at the extent of the damage to his friend's body. He was angry at himself for not having known Jelly Bean's first name.

For much of the time, the crew commander cried silently.

His name was Corporal Étienne Gonthier, known to his friends and to the world as Jelly Bean.

My heart is breaking.

Addendum, January 27, 2008: I have learned that my team from FOB Leopard were the ones who tried to revive Jelly Bean. That means they have been the responding medics for eight of Canada's eleven deaths on this tour. I can't help but worry about the effect this will have on them.

JANUARY 25 | Last Trip Home

We gather at the far end of the Taliban Last Stand (TLS) building (see the November 10–14 entry). Our company sergeant major, the senior non-commissioned officer of the group, organizes us into our ranks. When we are ready, we come to attention, turn to the left and march towards the waiting Hercules aircraft. Once we are close to the aircraft's ramp, we halt and turn to the right so that we are facing our comrades of the battle group.

After several minutes, a LAV drives onto the tarmac. The rear hatch is lowered. The coffin inside is removed by the pallbearers. These are chosen from among the dead soldier's buddies.

Before the pallbearers lift the coffin onto their shoulders, the padre (military chaplain) offers a prayer of remembrance. When the prayer is finished, we are called to attention again and given the order to salute. Every single person standing in the ranks does so. This is very different from any other parade. Normally, only the officer commanding the unit salutes. He or she is saluting for the group collectively. At a ramp ceremony, we are all saying goodbye individually.

At this point, the pallbearers place the coffin on their shoulders and make their way between the guards of honour. Every single Canadian currently at KAF who is not involved in vital work is standing there, as well as groups of other soldiers who are representing all the other nations serving in Afghanistan.

Following the pallbearers is the dead soldier's closest friend. He carries the dead man's beret. Following behind that is a bagpiper playing "Amazing Grace."

The hold of the Hercules is empty except for a stand on which the coffin will rest, two honour guards and a large Canadian flag.

The coffin is placed on the stand, and the pallbearers depart.

We turn to the right and march off. Once back at the TLS building, we are dismissed.

The ramp of the Hercules closes.

Jelly Bean is on his way home.

Normally, everybody leaves the tarmac after a ramp ceremony. This time, after we were dismissed, I decided to stay and watch as the Hercules made its way onto the runway.

Farewell, Jelly Bean.

I got word yesterday that my departure date, which for thirty-six hours had bounced between January 28 and February 12, has been confirmed for February 3. I can't wait to go home!

150

The change of departure date meant that this will be the second-last Saturday I spend at KAF. This is the day merchants come to the base to sell local goods and handicrafts. It is a popular stop with all the soldiers here. Because of my whirlwind departure, I had not had the chance to go before I left for the FOBs. I then learned that the market will be closed the following week, so it was now or never for the tourist thing.

I spent a very enjoyable couple of hours wandering around the various stalls and haggling. A good rule of thumb here, as elsewhere in the developing world, is to pay no more than half of the original asking price.

Even here, the war is never far away. The bazaar is on the edge of the base, and the entrance is guarded by a small detachment of soldiers armed with rifles and a medium machine gun. As well, the entire bazaar is surrounded by a double layer of barbed wire. At the edge of the bazaar, this leads to some interesting juxtapositions, such as a stack of Afghan dresses next to the barbed wire.

Even when you are well inside the bazaar, it is impossible to escape reality. A guard tower oversees the entire operation, and a variety of customers show up from all forty-plus countries in the Coalition—it's a challenge to recognize all the different combat uniforms.

The goods on sale here fall into two main categories: pottery and jewellery, and rugs and other textiles. The "war rug" shown in the first photograph is unique to Afghanistan. This country has been at war for so long that violent imagery has permeated into the fabric of life both literally and figuratively.

Like businessmen all over the world, these merchants sell whatever their customers are looking for. Obviously Christian images are available on carpets sold by obviously Muslim shopkeepers.

The haggling styles of the various merchants are remarkably distinctive. On the whole, they are more subdued than in similar markets I

A war rug

Christian imagery thrives in a Muslim market

have seen around the world.* A few merchants are even what you would call "soft sellers." I was particularly taken with one of them, a jewellery salesman. I ended up going back to his stall three times to get gifts—for my wife, my mother and my sister-in-law. This shy, even retiring, man works quite hard for his living. The same can be said for every other merchant at the bazaar. This is something Westerners sometimes have difficulty appreciating.

On my way back from the bazaar, I was offered a lift by a couple of Canadians. They asked about my purchases and about the price I had paid for the various items. One of them, a man older than me who should have known better, offered the opinion that the merchants I had purchased items from would be thrilled with their day's work because "twenty dollars is a year's income for these people."

Let me be absolutely clear here. Nowhere on earth is twenty dollars a year's income. Although economic data from these parts of the world are difficult to obtain and interpret, a Google-driven search reveals that Ethiopia, Malawi, Liberia and Somalia are tied for the lowest per capita income on the globe. In these countries, the poorest of the poor make something in the neighbourhood of two hundred dollars a year.

So what can you buy with a two-hundred-dollar annual income? Consider the elements that make up what we would call a good quality of life. A clean and spacious home; children who can be well fed, well clothed and educated; transportation to and from work; a varied diet. These things cost about the same no matter where you live. There is nothing magical about the developing world whereby the housing, transportation and food we would consider acceptable suddenly become much cheaper.

The difference in the developing world is that you can live marginally for far less than you can in Canada. For very little money, these people are able to access two or three basic foodstuffs every day

---

* This may have something to do with the fact that their clientele is heavily armed. How aggressive would you be with a customer carrying a C7 5.56 mm rifle that has an M203 grenade launcher attached to the barrel?

(generally high-carb, low-protein plants) and sleep in a place where they are sheltered from the wind and the rain. Even the homeless in Canada are unable to achieve that level of existence without an income several times greater than two hundred dollars.

This does not change the fact that the existence of people in the developing world is marginal at best. They live from day to day and from hand to mouth. If anything untoward happens, such as illness, the loss of a domesticated animal or a fire in a part of the family shelter, the effect is catastrophic. The survival of an entire family can be threatened by such an event. There are none of the elements of the social safety net that we take for granted in Canada.

You will often see Westerners get upset in a developing-world market because someone paid ninety-five dollars for the same item they bought for a hundred dollars. Perhaps reading the above four paragraphs would make them feel better.

JANUARY 28 | Kandahar Kanadiana

No description of the Canadian KAF experience would be complete without a thorough description of the local Tim Hortons. It is reputedly the single most successful Tim's franchise anywhere in the world. The salient facts of this operation are as follows:

1. There are nine staff members. Two of these are assigned exclusively to baking. All nine work every single day they are here, on tours that generally last six months. The money they make is, in the words of one of them, "ridiculously good."

2. The hours of operation are 0600–2100. There is always a lineup, except between the hours of 1130–1230 and 1730–1830, when most people are eating their meals. The line moves very slowly because people are frequently buying twenty to thirty coffees at a time, as they are buying for their entire unit. The staff has even taken large orders

Canadian culture

like this from soldiers about to go to a FOB. These orders are usually preceded by the question: "What travels well?" I can imagine that there would be no better morale-booster on a FOB than to receive a Tim's doughnut.

3. There are 10 coffee brewers going full time. These brewers will produce over 10,000 cups of coffee a day. The population of KAF varies between 12,000 and 14,000.

4. Over 500 doughnuts will be sold before 1000 each day.

5. The store sells 50 times more French vanilla coffee than any other Tim's outlet. This flavour is sold almost exclusively to British soldiers. Go figure.

6. You can come into the store, or you can be served at a walk-by window!

It took quite a bit of doing to get the photo of "Canadian culture." The Tim's is so busy that every time I walked by, hoping to snap the shot, there were far too many people around. I finally resorted to sneaking out of the Role 3 Hospital at mid-morning and running over during one of the lulls in the action (the Tim's action, that is). And despite a strong desire to partake of their products, I never got to taste anything produced by Pizza Hut Kandahar or Burger King Kandahar—the lineups were always far too long. North Americans and their junk food—an addiction not easily broken.

JANUARY 30 | Emergency Department Echo—Kandahar

In one of my very first entries in this diary, I mentioned that the physicians here were very keen to have me teach them about bedside ultrasound. They had always intended to ask me to run an ultrasound course before I left; my time at the FOBs had only delayed things. I have finally taught the course over the past two weeks, breaking it up into individual lectures.

I'm quite pleased to be able to report to you that the following pictures are from the final session of EDE Course #300—Emergency Department Echo Kandahar. We had Danish, Dutch, British, Australian and American participants, as well as Canadians! I was even able to teach my company commander, Major Jocelyn Dodaro, a few things.*

I realize I haven't written much about the medicine I have practised here at KAF since my return from the FOBs. There have been three separate multiple-patient incidents since my return. EDE played an important role in two of these.

---

* It was particularly satisfying for me to be able to teach Major Dodaro. It was because of his confidence in me that I had been sent outside the wire. Throughout my time at the FOBs, he had been a constant source of support and wise advice. He even came to visit me (by land!) at FOB Leopard. The FOB medical team was lucky to have a man like this leading us.

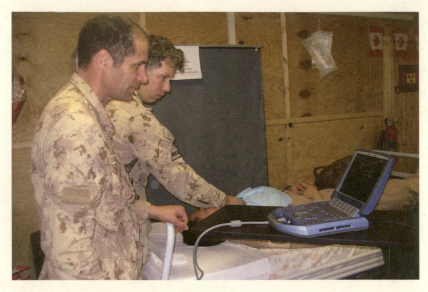

Role reversal—teaching my company commander

In the first, the patient had arrived after an IED blast with severe leg wounds. He had a very low blood pressure on arrival, so we quickly resuscitated him with intravenous fluids and got him into the operating room.

A chest X-ray, which was done before he went to the operating room, had appeared normal except for some broken ribs. As well, bedside ultrasound examinations of his abdomen and chest did not reveal any bleeding. However, approximately an hour into the operation, he continued to have a low blood pressure and his hemoglobin had dropped alarmingly. It is wise, when a patient deteriorates, to re-examine him or her completely. As the patient was now under general anesthesia with one orthopedic surgeon working on each leg, it would have been very difficult to take him to the CT scanner. I offered to go into the operating room to re-examine his abdomen and chest with ultrasound. Not surprisingly, I found that he had lost a great deal of blood into his chest, on the side the ribs were broken. The chest surgeon was called to deal with this.

This patient also developed another problem. When we give a lot of different kinds of fluids in the immediate resuscitation of such a patient, it is not unusual for the patient's blood to have difficulty clotting (INR 3.4, for the medical types). When this happens, even small wounds (like intravenous punctures) can bleed a lot. Our dilemma was that we needed to start a large IV line in the jugular vein of the neck to give him even more fluids more quickly, to correct his low blood pressure.* This can be very dangerous for the patient. If the intravenous needle cuts the jugular vein (rather than threading itself into it), patients can bleed so much into the neck (because they are clotting poorly) that their windpipe will be crushed

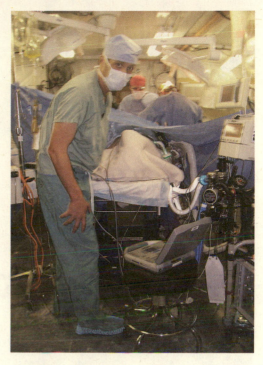

EDE in the O.R.

and they will suffocate. If the carotid artery is cut, the same thing can happen even more quickly. This can occur because the carotid artery lies right beside (sometimes right behind) the jugular vein. Hitting the artery can also cause a stroke if the blood flow to the brain is interrupted. Finally, there is the risk that you will miss the vein *and* the artery and hit the lung instead, causing it to collapse. You want to get this procedure right the first time.

Fortunately, I was again able to assist with bedside ultrasound by precisely locating where the jugular vein was and guiding the intravenous needle into it on the first attempt. This was particularly useful in this patient because his jugular vein was far more to the side than it is in most patients. The civilian anaesthetist had trouble believing that I wanted to put the needle where I did, but I could show him on the ultrasound screen that the jugular vein was *right there.*

---

* For the medical types: femoral access would have been very challenging due to the ongoing bilateral orthopedic procedures.

If you arrive alive, you will survive

To the best of my knowledge, this is the first time an emergency physician has gone into an operating room to use bedside ultrasound to assist in the management of a patient.

The second case involved another IED victim. He also had lost a considerable amount of blood from his leg wounds and arrived in profound shock with a very low blood pressure. He had no apparent wounds above the waist, and his abdomen was soft and not painful. But in an episode reminiscent of the one with the Afghan soldier at FOB Leopard (see the January 3 entry), bedside ultrasound confirmed the presence of abdominal bleeding. Knowing this, we proceeded immediately to abdominal surgery after packing and binding his leg wounds and controlling the bleeding coming from there. During the abdominal surgery, wounds to the spleen and stomach were repaired. With the patient now stabilized, the orthopedic surgeons took over and fixed his legs.

Without our knowing that the patient was bleeding in the abdomen, it might have been tempting to send him to the orthopedic surgeons directly. Had this happened, the abdominal bleeding might only have been detected much later, perhaps leading to a poorer outcome.

I also went into the O.R. for this case to help get an intravenous line started. The patient's blood pressure was so low that the nurses had been unable to find a vein on his arms. The anesthetist tried to start an IV in the big vein in the groin but missed. Once again using bedside ultrasound guidance, I was able to place a line on the first attempt in the jugular vein in the neck. The anesthetist was very grateful.

All in all, the care given to patients here matches or exceeds that afforded in any Level 1 Trauma Centre in Canada. For that reason, the motto of the MMU is "if you arrive alive, you will survive." If you get to KAF with a pulse, you will almost certainly go home alive.

JANUARY 31 (Day) | Outside the Wire One Last Time

The reward for good work is . . . more work.

The bedside ultrasound course I finished teaching a few days ago went over so well that one of the American participants asked me to spend a day at a hospital they have built at a large base a few kilometres from KAF. The base consists of FOB Lion (American-run) and Camp Hero (run by the ANA). The hospital, which opened approximately a month ago, is for the exclusive use of the ANA. When it is fully operational, it will serve the needs of the ANA brigade based at Camp Hero and will assist in the management of Afghan casualties arriving at KAF. It will take some time for the hospital to reach this level of functionality, but we obviously want the Afghans to be self-sufficient in medical as well as military resources. I was thrilled with the assignment because it would give me a chance to see yet more of the country and, especially, it would give me a chance to interact with more Afghans directly ("Teach a man to fish . . ." etc.). I was a little less thrilled when I found out that, since this was an ANA gig, I would be making the trip in an unarmoured pickup truck.

My ride for the day

When we got to FOB Lion, I climbed one of the guard towers to look around. While there, I could not resist having my picture taken with an American soldier whose last name (Boozer) must earn him a lot of ribbing, considering the complete absence of alcohol in the Afghan theatre of operations. And do you see what I meant earlier? Be honest. I look like a dork with a helmet on, don't I?

As the Americans are temporarily without a radiologist to act as mentor to the Afghans, they asked me to spend the day with their ultrasound technician. He had taken a six-month course in ultrasound in Kabul but hadn't had any exposure to trauma or first-trimester pregnancy applications.

I had been told that he was "the smartest guy in the hospital," and he lived up to his advance billing. He was very sharp, easy to teach and quick to learn. However, he showed a pattern one often sees in medical professionals trained in the developing world. Medical teaching in these countries is still extremely hierarchical. The teacher expects the students to learn his particular area of expertise in excruciating detail, while ignoring almost everything else.

The dork in the helmet

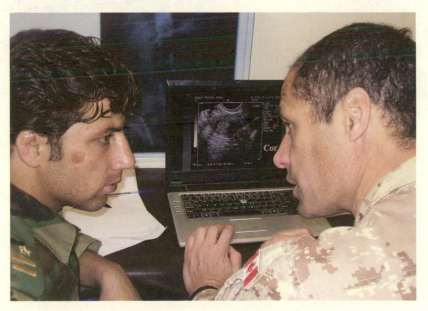

Sharp and quick to learn

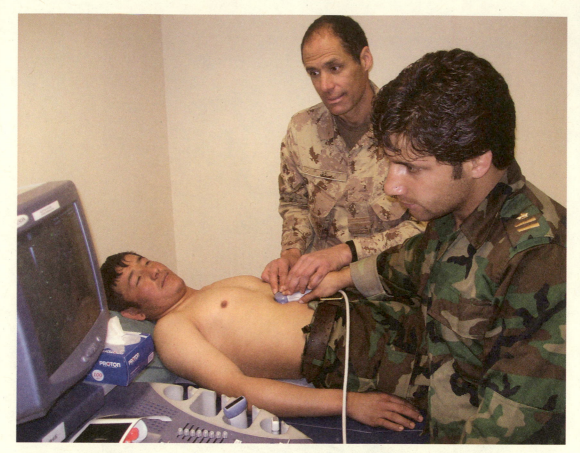

New skills for my Afghan colleague

Because of this, there were certain areas where his knowledge was solid. At other times, the concept I was introducing was completely new to him. Having said that, he was able to build on existing knowledge and asked very pertinent questions every step of the way.* I spent the whole day with him going over all of the basic and advanced bedside ultrasound material I had with me. I hope he found it useful.

---

* He had the unnerving habit of preceding every question with a quite loud "SIR!" As I said, medical teaching in the developing world is very hierarchical.

On my way back from the FOB, I stopped in at the hospital to let them know I was safely back "inside the wire." I was about to leave when we received a request for telephone advice. I was the only doctor present, so I took the call. An ANA vehicle checkpoint close by had had an episode that goes by the ominous name of "escalation of force." A driver was ordered to halt. When he did not do so, warning shots were fired. When this did not have the desired effect, the checkpoint guards shot to kill.

The caller stated that the driver had been shot in the shoulder. I asked about his condition and was assured he was stable. The checkpoint commander requested that we send an ambulance to retrieve the wounded man. This would have been a bad idea, as the ambulances at KAF are not armoured and are never used outside the wire. They only retrieve patients from the medevac choppers or deliver them to the planes that will take them to Landstuhl (see the November 18 entry) or Canada.

I sensed that the information concerning the patient might be inaccurate, so I ordered the checkpoint people to throw the wounded man into whatever vehicle they had, and to rush in. Meanwhile, I would organize an ambulance to meet them at the KAF gate.

Ten minutes later I received a report from our ambulance crew, who had taken over the care of the patient at the gate. The patient either had dramatically worsened en route or had not been properly examined at the scene. He was now in cardiac arrest, and the ambulance crew was performing CPR.

Given the penetrating nature of the injury, I had the surgical team paged urgently and prepared to perform an emergency thoracotomy, also known as "cracking the chest." This means that I got a big scalpel with which to open the chest on the left side, rib spreaders with which to expose the heart and the left lung, and a clamp with which to squeeze shut the big artery that comes off the heart and goes down to the abdomen and legs. By doing this, one keeps whatever blood the patient still has inside him circulating between his heart and lungs and brain. This can buy you a few minutes to stave off what is otherwise an inevitable death due to blood loss, and get the patient into the operating room.

When the patient arrived, it seemed that any resuscitation attempt would be futile. The pupils were fixed and in a midrange position, which is worse than being fully dilated. Despite the grim prognosis, we still gave it our best. A colleague intubated the patient (put a breathing tube into his lungs so that we could get him on a ventilator) while the nurses started IVs and I took a look at the heart and lungs with the bedside ultrasound machine. Although the scan was technically difficult to do, it did not seem that there was any bleeding around the heart. This can cause pressure to build up around the heart, crushing the heart and making it impossible for it to pump blood. In these cases it is necessary to either stick a big needle into the heart to relieve the pressure or to perform the "chest cracking" manoeuvre described above.

Another easily correctable cause of cardiac arrest in this setting is bleeding into the chest. This can be so massive that it can also crush the heart, again making it impossible for the heart to pump blood. As the ultrasound exam was indeterminate, I took my scalpel and cut into the chest on the side he was wounded until I was through the rib muscles. I then stuck my finger into the chest and made a large hole in the chest wall. Very little blood came out. Had there been a strong gush of blood, it would have been possible that the patient was bleeding into the chest as described above. Unfortunately, this was not the case. Rather, it seemed he had bled out. I took another look at the heart with bedside ultrasound. There were no signs of cardiac activity. I suggested that we stop our resuscitation efforts, and no one objected.

When bullets go through a body, they expand. This causes the hole where they exit to be much larger than the hole where they entered. It was obvious that the large wound in the left shoulder was an exit wound where a bullet had come out. On the patient's back we found two smaller punctures, consistent with rifle bullets. It is therefore possible that this man was shot while turning, if not frankly fleeing the scene. Whether or not this implied guilt on his part will probably never be proven beyond doubt, unless documents or weapons are found in the vehicle. What is certain is that failure to obey a checkpoint in Afghanistan in 2008 is highly suspicious. Everybody knows that fingers are on triggers and that SVBIEDs (suicide vehicle–borne IEDs) have made checkpoint guards very cautious. You have to be crazy or guilty to disobey them.

Although our efforts were unsuccessful, we gave this probable enemy soldier the best care we could. This care and respect continues after death. One of our interpreters, who is a lay preacher in the Afghan community, was called to the bedside. He pronounced the Muslim prayers for the departed while wearing the correct religious accoutrements. He then performed the various rituals dictated by Afghan Islam for the preparation of the body.

We do this because we are fighting this war in a moral manner.

FEBRUARY 1 | Dinner with the Lads

I was overjoyed to learn, when I returned from Camp Hero yesterday, that my team from FOB Leopard was back in town and that they had come looking for me at the Role 3 Hospital. I tracked them down today to invite them out to dinner.

The lads were in fine spirits when I caught up to them. They had been given four days in KAF, two of which were completely off. They would have to work in the Role 1 facility the other two days.

I took them out to the only true restaurant on the base. I had mentioned earlier that the Burger King, Subway and Pizza Hut outlets were no more than "walk-through" windows. In this place, you get to sit down at a non-cafeteria–style table. The lighting is not the harsh glare of the DFac cafeteria. And (drum roll, please) you get to eat with metal utensils! I don't think I mentioned this detail earlier: the DFacs only have plastic cutlery. The same is true for the mess tents at the FOBs. After three months, eating with cheap plastic gets pretty old.

You won't believe this but the name of the place is . . . Echos. Yet another allusion to ultrasound, you ask? Nope. It's a Dutch abbreviation of some kind. The place is run by a religious group from Holland whose goal is to "foster contact between military and civilians."

Hmmm. A religious group trying to improve the morale of the troops? You might walk in here expecting a warm and fuzzy embrace from restaurant staff. What you get, unfortunately, is lousy food provided to you by people who seem to go out of their way to make it clear that they despise you. You, personally. The person taking your order could not seem less interested in what you have to say. The person providing the food barks your order number out in a manner reminiscent of a drill sergeant calling a platoon to attention. And woe betide the customer foolish enough to ask for the order to be explained. When Mike (the medic) asked which two milkshakes were banana and which one was vanilla (they were all white), he almost got his head ripped off.

"Look! Two of them are banana! One is vanilla! That's what you ordered, right? Right!?"

I had to walk over there to rescue him. It should tell you how sick we are of plastic utensils and harsh lighting that we were able to see this as entertainment and still thoroughly enjoy ourselves.

The conversation was about what you would expect. We talked mostly about the two guys who had been killed after I had left the FOB. Much of what we talked about is too sensitive, either militarily or personally, to discuss in much detail here. What is important is that I was able to feel, one more time, that incredible camaraderie that comes between people who have been together in a war zone.

As intense as these relationships are, however, they are no different from any other. With enough months and miles, the intensity fades. Life goes on, and new relationships are formed. The person you swore you would keep in touch with for the rest of your life fades from your memory. When you get together, after many years, you are overjoyed to see your old brother-in-arms. The problem is that you haven't maintained the relationship during the intervening time, so the only thing the two of you can talk about is the past. Every sentence starts with the words "Do you remember . . . ?" When you run out of things you remember, you haven't got anything to talk about. Often that's the last

The Four Musketeers, with swords crossed

time you see each other, because you realize the relationship that meant so much to you during the war is now behind you. This has been the case for me and those I was with in the Central American and African wars I have lived through.

I'm going to do my best not to let this happen to the four of us. I have an advantage here in that, as Quebecers, they are limited in how far they are likely to roam across Canada. As well, my Québécois wife likes nothing better than an excuse to go back to her home province. Finally, I have that tool that has transformed our ability to stay in contact with our friends: e-mail. Since I started e-mailing over ten years ago, I have managed not only to stay in touch with every new friend I have made but also to reconnect with old friends I had completely lost touch with, some of them for over a decade.

So before we broke up, I made sure we had a plan. I will take my family to Quebec City the next time Gino is playing the guitar for one of his wife's flamenco presentations. I will stay in touch with Mike as he deliberates over whether to go to medical school. Once Frank decides what he will be doing after he returns home, he will let us all know so that we can look him up whenever we are in Quebec City.

We'll see how that goes.

Addendum, March 15, 2009: It has gone fairly well! We have exchanged a number of e-mails. I got together with the entire team last summer, when I brought my family to Quebec City for the 400th anniversary of the founding of the city. While we were there, I also got to see Gino play the guitar for one of his wife's classes. Just before Christmas, Mike was able to come to Sudbury for a weekend (he had been on a course at Canadian Forces Base Borden, just a little ways south of Sudbury). And just last night, after doing some advanced bedside ultrasound teaching for the PAs and doctors deploying next month, I was able to get together with Gino and Mike again, as well as with Bubu and Christian from FOB Lynx. They are all living in or near Quebec City, so I invited them out to a great little restaurant in the old city.

We had a blast! To my delight, Christian remembered many of the bedside ultrasound notions I had taught him at the FOB (see the December 10 entry). We laughed and cried about what we had gone through together, but we also talked about the future. Mike is about to become a father; Gino is considering applying to the physician assistant program; Bubu is teaching younger medics and may go back to Afghanistan in 2010; Christian is nicely settled in with a three-year full-time contract with his reserve unit.

As we left the restaurant, we passed by a bar with an enormous lineup. It was March break in Ontario, and hundreds of college-age kids were waiting to get into the place. Several of them were remarkably attractive young women, so the boys stood there watching for a few minutes, as soldiers have since the dawn of time. I could not help looking at my old teammates and reflecting on the fact that, although they looked just as young as the kids lined up outside the bar, they were separated from them by their experience of war. I wondered if any of the kids waiting to party that night could understand what these men had been through. The answer is almost certainly no. But we understood. And that is what is most important to us.

I look forward to keeping in touch with these guys for many years to come.

After dinner, I reported back to the Role 3 Hospital. Although I had been given today and tomorrow off to prepare for my departure on February 3, I volunteered to do the night shift for my friend Aaron, one of the U.S. physicians who works at the MMU. American doctors deployed to Afghanistan stay here for fifteen months. I figured my friend deserved a break.

The evening started off with a bang with a visit by General Walter Natynczyk, the vice chief of defence staff (VCDS), the number two soldier in our entire armed forces. The leadership of the Canadian Forces takes a very active interest in the troops in Afghanistan, and we are regularly visited by them. The general in charge of all CF forces deployed overseas came to FOB Lynx while I was there and held a meeting with the entire combat team. He wanted to hear our complaints, and he heard them! He genuinely engaged the troops. Unfortunately, there was another general who, after representatives of every unit on the FOB were gathered in the mess tent to meet him, did not show up. Nor did he ever send an explanation for his failure to arrive. I felt that this showed a deplorable lack of respect for the combat troops.

General Walter Natynczyk promotes a private

I am therefore pleased to be able to say that the VCDS acquitted himself very well. He was (almost) punctual, he took the time to shake each and every hand there, and his words to the group afterwards were heartfelt, sincere and very validating.

He ended his visit by promoting one of our privates (the bottom-most rank in the army) to the rank of corporal (the first step up). Normally, this promotion would be awarded by, at best, a middle-ranking officer. To have one's corporal stripes put on by a general, and a very senior one at that, was quite a thrill for the young soldier.

It is now a little bit past midnight. Tonight has been utterly quiet. Just one Filipino patient with benign positional vertigo (dizziness). The only excitement has been generated by a torrential rain, which has flooded several rooms in the hospital complex. My office has had to be mopped twice already, and the rain shows no signs of abating.

In a few more hours, I will have officially completed my duties as a medical officer with Task Force Afghanistan.

Addendum, June 10, 2008: General Natynczyk has been made chief of defence staff (CDS)—the top soldier for the entire Canadian Forces. If this book ever makes it to him, I hope he forgives that "almost punctual" crack! Seriously, it should make every Canadian feel proud and secure that a fairly lowly soldier (a captain—me) feels absolutely no need to clear what I have written with the top dog. The Canadian Forces is not in the business of censoring what its soldiers say, except when it comes to operational security issues. Compare that with the zero criticism tolerated by totalitarian regimes, even from the press. We live in a great country.

FEBRUARY 2 | Reflections on a Moral War

My last full day in Afghanistan. This is a time for reflection, an attempt to summarize what I have learned. The best place to start is with my first letter, where I stated that there have been very few wars fought for a moral ideal. I also pointed out that, over the years, there have been moral reasons for going to war that our nation has not acted upon.

Consider the Rwandan genocide. It is unique in the butcheries of the twentieth century in that it was remarkably low-tech. Nearly a million human beings were slaughtered in a few months by murderers armed mostly with machetes. Would it not have been moral for Canada, even unilaterally, to send combat troops to stop these killers? It certainly would have been a lot easier than what we are doing in Afghanistan. Similarly, the genocidal Janjaweed militia in Darfur could be crushed by the Canadian Battle Group deployed in Kandahar without any assistance from NATO allies. Would it not be moral to do so?

Some people question the appropriateness of armed force in humanitarian disasters. But if you saw a group of men beating someone on the street, would you call the police? If it is moral to call on men with guns to use potentially lethal force in this situation, then it must be moral to do so for other citizens of the world who are being abused. The cries for help from Afghanistan are hard to hear, but it is still moral to answer them.

Of course, other parts of the world are equally deserving of the attention of the Canadian army. Some people question why we are in Afghanistan when there are other areas where we could probably do more good with the same amount of effort. The most commonly mentioned case here is Darfur, but for various geopolitical reasons we cannot intervene militarily there. For other geopolitical reasons, some of them good and some of them ambiguous, Canada is in a position to intervene in Afghanistan. The question is not where we will use armed force; it is whether or not we participate in the Afghan mission. To wait until we are sure that we are addressing only the "most deserving" situation is a guarantee that we will never do anything to counter injustice. The debate over which cause is "most deserving" would paralyze our body politic.

The only question our nation should be debating is whether the Afghan war is a moral one. If it is, then our course is clear and the objections being advanced lose their validity.

For instance, we are hearing a lot about the need for more combat troops to fight alongside the Canadians in Kandahar. Many people argue that we should pull out if we can't get more countries to do their share of the heavy lifting.

Can you imagine making that argument in the summer of 1940? Hitler effectively controlled all of Western Europe. Britain stood alone against the Nazis. Yet we sent every single man we could to join Churchill.

Can you imagine making that argument in the winter of 1942? The Japanese militarists, fuelled by an ideology of racial superiority no less abhorrent than that of the Nazis, had swept everything before them in the Pacific. The Nazis, meanwhile, were deep inside the Soviet Union. Things looked even worse than they had in 1940. We fought on regardless.

There were probably many Canadians who, faced with these seemingly impossible odds, wondered whether we would ever prevail. We continued to fight because the destruction of our enemies was a moral imperative. The world could not tolerate the continued existence of Auschwitz and Unit 731 (the little-remembered Japanese group that did much the same things to the Koreans and the Chinese that the Nazis did to the Jews).

The other thing that is clear to me is that I was bang on when I described my goals for this mission: to keep the Taliban at bay long enough to allow Afghanistan to educate its people.

I said much the same thing about Communism the last time I was in uniform, over a quarter century ago. I have always been of a somewhat socialist bent, so I was able to see the redeeming qualities of our Cold War enemies. Although oppressive regimes closely resemble each other in their violence, insecurity and hypocrisy no matter where they lie on the political spectrum, they differ markedly in their attitude towards education. Right-wing dictatorships generally treat their people like cattle. They prefer to keep them uneducated. Left-wing dictatorships, on the other hand, educate their people. I always felt this was Communism's Achilles heel. By educating their people, they sowed the seeds of their own destruction. It is inconceivable that the wave of liberation which swept through Eastern Europe in 1989 would have occurred in an illiterate population. We won the Cold War by continually confronting the Communists until education destroyed them from within.

The same thing has to happen here. We have to stay in Afghanistan long enough to get a majority of the population educated to a high school level or better. This would be the single greatest bulwark against the return of Taliban extremism. It will take several years and a continuation of our combat mission for the time being. The Taliban realize that educated people will reject them, so they threaten and kill students and teachers, particularly female ones. We have to stay to protect them.

In my first letter, I also stated that the "muscular" peacekeeping operations in Bosnia and East Timor as well as the NATO combat mission against the Serbs in Kosovo represented a positive evolution in the way armed force is used on this planet. I wrote that Afghanistan represented the next step in that evolution, and everything I have seen here has convinced me that this analysis was correct. Being war, the situation will be fraught with imperfections. But this is where the liberal democracies of the world have taken a stand against extremism. Canada must not sit out any part of this fight.

Finally, I will point out yet again that this is a war of ideas. Liberal democracy, for all its faults and problems, is a far better idea than is a system that believes it is acceptable to send people, often mentally deficient ones, to die in suicide bombings which kill more children than targets (see <http://www.cbc.ca/world/story/2008/02/19/iraq-baghdad.html>). Our enemies believe this is acceptable because the children will have died furthering the cause of the bombers. There is no way that idea can survive. There is no way it should.

To back away now would be to fail in the single noblest undertaking Canada has participated in since the end of World War Two. It would mean admitting that those who want to follow an extremist, nihilistic path have only to hold on long enough and we will eventually leave them alone. It would mean that Nico, Jelly Bean and all the others had died in vain. Please help me make sure that does not happen.

If this diary has convinced you that our involvement here is moral, then tell people that. If you are still not convinced, keep reading about

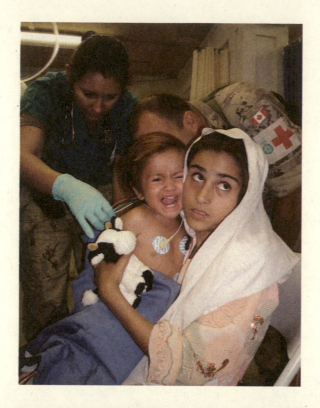

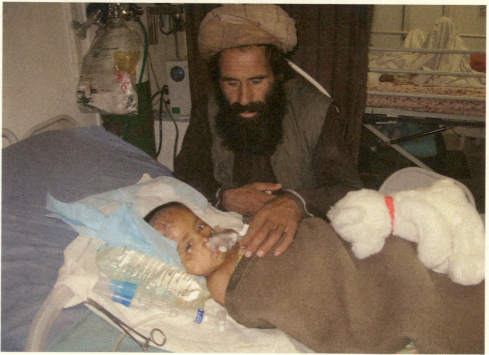

Treating Afghan children wounded by Taliban IEDS

the mission from whatever sources you trust. Democracies need informed citizens if they are to make sound choices.

And if you remain opposed to the mission, I will always respect that. I sincerely believe we will beat the Taliban for the same reason we beat the Nazis and then the Communists: our ideas are fundamentally more appealing than theirs. One of those ideas, perhaps the most important of all, is tolerance for other points of view.

FEBRUARY 3 | Leaving KAF

The schedule for Hercules aircraft leaving KAF being highly variable, I was quite pleased to learn that I wouldn't be flying out until late in the afternoon. This gave me the chance to make one last round of good-byes. As with my departure from FOB Leopard, these were melancholy moments. I couldn't wait to be on my way, but at the same time I realized that one of the most significant experiences of my life was coming to an end.

We started with a late brunch at the Echos restaurant with many of the physicians from the MMU. I followed this with a visit to the Role 1 and Role 3 facilities, saying goodbye to as many of the support staff as possible and hearing the inevitable "Did you hear? Your tour got extended!" joke that is almost *de rigueur* whenever someone leaves.

Although I haven't spoken much about them in this diary, I was very impressed with the senior officers of the MMU. To honour them, I did something that was technically inappropriate: as I came by their offices to say goodbye, I came to attention in front of their desks and snapped off a perfect salute.

For the civilians out there, a short explanation is required. KAF is considered "the field" when it comes to saluting. This means that, while proper respect is paid to superiors, even General Rick Hillier is not saluted when he is here. The reason for this is quite practical. By saluting someone, you are alerting any sniper in the area that the person being saluted is a high-value target. Since we were inside buildings, I was able

Visiting the KAF cenotaph

to honour my commanders without having them incur any undue risk. I hope they enjoyed the gesture.

The colonel commanding the MMU returned the favour a few hours later by presenting me with the MMU coin. The military types reading this will know how special this is, and it was a great moment for me. Then it was back to the shack one last time to do a final e-mail check and finish packing, and a last visit to the KAF cenotaph to pay my respects. Then it was off to the airfield and back onto a Herc.

You may recall that the first lines of the *Lonely Planet Afghanistan* were: "By any stretch of the imagination, Afghanistan isn't the simplest country to travel in." The second paragraph begins: "With the right preparations, and a constant ear to the ground once you're there, travel in Afghanistan is not only a possibility but also incredibly rewarding."

I doubt the *Lonely Planet* staff had my kind of "trip" in mind when they wrote that, but it certainly applies to the last three months. Difficult, uncomfortable, heartbreaking at times. And among the most rewarding things I have ever done.

Goodbye, Kandahar

FEBRUARY 4 | Emptying My Pockets

I am now back at Camp Mirage, our staging base "somewhere in the Middle East" (see my November 10–14 entry). I turned in my weapons today. As I predicted, it doesn't feel the least bit odd to be unarmed. On the contrary, it feels normal. I also turned in the ammunition I had been issued. The bullets were still in the magazines I had loaded before boarding the chopper that had taken me to FOB Lynx . . . except for two of them.

Medallions from my mother   Two bullets, just in case

The entire time I was outside the wire I carried, in the left pocket of my combat pants, four medallions my mother had sent me.

In my right pocket, I carried two bullets, one for my pistol and one for my rifle. This practice is not unusual for Canadian soldiers in Afghanistan. If by some incredible stroke of bad luck, most likely due to a helicopter crash, it looked like I was going to be captured by the Taliban and I ran out of ammunition, I wanted to have the option to end my life painlessly.*

If you could see what our enemies do to their prisoners, you would probably do the same thing.

FEBRUARY 7 | Decompression

Ten days before I was to leave KAF, I was told that because I had spent so much time "outside the wire" I had to go to something called TLD (third location decompression) before being allowed to go home. At first, I found this disappointing and frustrating. I just wanted to get back to my

---

* My best friend from medical school, a psychiatrist, has explained to me that this was an attempt to regain control—through suicide—over a situation where I was about to lose all control through capture and torture. All I could think of at the time was that I did not want to suffer that much before dying.

Time to decompress and reflect

family. Having been here a couple of days, though, I have to admit that the army is doing a very good thing.

Although I think I have come through this experience with a minimum of psychic scars, the last few days have been quite beneficial. Returning directly to Sudbury from KAF might have been a little jarring. That was certainly the case for me twenty years ago (almost to the day), when I returned from the Nicaraguan war. That time, I went from being shot at in the jungle to landing at Toronto's Pearson International Airport in less than thirty-six hours. My youth and relative inexperience certainly played a part, but I remember being shaky for a few weeks after I got back.

So here I am, in a five-star hotel on the shores of the Indian Ocean. Thank you, Canadian taxpayer!

The only thing that is a little strange is that virtually everyone else who is here with me worked in the headquarters units at KAF. All of the people at the FOBs and at the MMU will be going through the process a few weeks later. I find myself spending almost all my time on my own. Perhaps that is best.

Back at Camp Mirage. We leave for the airport in a couple of hours. I'll be home tomorrow.

I am happy, but there is none of the excitement that going home after a long absence usually generates. The reason is obvious. Not all of us are going home.

If you have ever lost someone close to you, you have probably experienced the feeling that they are going to walk around the corner any minute now. It's a feeling that is both agonizingly sad and yet almost pleasant, because your heart keeps hoping that the loss was a mistake, that your loved one is really all right. While that feeling lasts, you don't have to fully accept that your buddy is dead. I am experiencing a fair bit of that now.

Two of the twelve men lost on this rotation, Master Corporal Nicholas "Nico" Beauchamp and Master Corporal Christian "Conan" Duchesne,* were medics—a far higher proportion than statistics would have predicted. This should not be a surprise. The combat medics I worked with were not only incredibly competent, they also were 100 per cent committed to looking after their buddies, even at the risk of their own lives. The CF is committed to delivering the highest level of health care possible to its troops in battle, and it is the combat medics who put that commitment into action. They are the ones who live—and die—by the motto of the Health Services: "*Militi Succurrimus*—We Aid the Soldier." I am honoured to have worn the same badge on my beret as these men.

Badge of the CF Health Services

* Master Corporal Duchesne was killed on August 22, 2007. He died in an IED strike that also killed the most senior man to die on my rotation: Master Warrant Officer Mario Mercier.

In previous rotations, two other medics were killed in action: Corporal Glen Arnold and Corporal Andrew "Boomer" Eykelenboom. Corporal Arnold, of McKerrow, Ontario, died in the same suicide attack that killed Private David Byers (see my December 18 entry). Byers came from Espanola. McKerrow and Espanola, which are about five kilometres apart, are just outside my hometown of Sudbury. No other city has lost two men on the same day since the Korean War. For this to occur in such a small place—where everybody knows each other—must have been devastating.

And so I sit here in the Camp Mirage mess hall, waiting for Nico . . . or Conan . . . or Boomer . . . or Glen . . . to come around the corner.

Addendum, December 5, 2008: The commitment of the combat medics to their duty—and the price they pay for that commitment—remains unchanged. During the recently completed Roto 5, two more medics were killed in action: Corporal Michael Starker, KIA May 6, 2008, and Private Colin Wilmot, KIA July 6, 2008.

FEBRUARY 9 | Home

There is one vital aspect of my Afghanistan experience that I have not yet described.

When a soldier goes to war, his entire family goes with him.* My daughter, Michelle, is still too young to have a sense of time. Apart from throwing a few temper tantrums during the first weeks of my tour, she adjusted to my absence fairly well. My wife, Claude, on the other hand, felt each day of my mission acutely.

Everyone who knows me knows I am a dreamer. As I have chased my dreams for the past twelve years, Claude has been a constant

---

* *Postscript, March 3, 2009:* It seems that my musings travelled even farther in the corridors of power than I had dared to hope! Today, more than a year after I wrote these words, U.S. First Lady Michelle Obama appeared on CNN to say, "When our soldiers go to war, their families go with them."

support for me. Nothing makes this clearer than a conversation we had last April. We were in a restaurant in Montreal, discussing our future. It was evident that the EDE course would soon be able to go off on its own. There were now eight fully trained teams capable of giving the course independently. The task that had consumed my life for seven years was winding down, and we were looking forward to my spending more time at home.

We had not discussed the possibility of my going to Afghanistan yet, but she had seen me follow every detail of the mission since it had begun. She had seen me cheer our government's decision to send troops in the first place. She had heard me argue in favour of the mission. She had seen me suffer every time our soldiers were killed or wounded.

I had met a military doctor at a conference in March 2007, and that meeting crystallized the feelings I had for the mission into a firm desire to do my part in it. When I told Claude that there was one more thing I needed to do before I slowed down, she looked me right in the eye and said: "You want to go to Afghanistan, don't you?"

When I said yes, her eyes got moist, but she smiled and looked at me and said, "I'm not surprised. And I completely support you." This was one of those magical moments in our relationship. We felt we understood each other perfectly and felt completely connected to each other.

Unfortunately, that magical moment only lasted about thirty seconds. Michelle—who was not yet two years old—decided to express what she thought of the idea of her father going to war by projectile vomiting all over herself and the restaurant table. When we went to the car to get fresh clothes for her, we discovered that we had been robbed of our laptops, digital cameras, backpacks and one bedside ultrasound machine. What could have been a wonderful "couple" evening was spent filing a police report. But I digress.

It is important to realize that Claude spent much more time confronting the possibility of my death than I did. There were many times when our telephone conversations were cut off because of the vagaries of satellite communications. Each time this happened, Claude had to consider the possibility that the conversation had been ended by a lethal rocket strike.

Home!

The fact is that throughout this mission I have gotten tremendous family support. This is important in any relationship, and so much more so when one is in a war zone. To be able to find comfort at the end of a satellite phone line or from an e-mail from the woman you love makes all the difference. I am a very lucky man.

FEBRUARY 11 | Father and Child Reunion

Claude and I had agreed that we would meet in Toronto and spend a few days with each other before I came home to Sudbury. The scene at the Sudbury airport was, as anticipated, a bit of a zoo: my parents, my brother and his family, various friends, reporters and TV crews all showed up. I had not wanted to expose Michelle to that on her first contact with me, so we arranged for her to stay at home with her uncle.

Reunion

We timed my arrival home for the end of her nap. When we heard her waking up, Claude and I went into her room. She looked up at me and smiled, just a little. Then she went towards her mother. We then went into the living room, where Claude and Michelle sat on one couch while I sat across the room from them. Claude and I just talked quietly.

After about twenty minutes, Michelle came over to me and got on my lap.

Nothing is harder for a soldier who goes to war than leaving a young child behind. Nothing is more pleasant for a soldier returning from war than having that child welcome you back.

MARCH 3 | Supporting the War

I first approached the Canadian Forces to volunteer for service in Afghanistan in the spring of 2007. Although it would have involved far less paperwork (and been far more lucrative) to go as a civilian, it was very important for me that I do this as a soldier. I wanted it to be crystal clear that I believed in the mission and that I was willing to take the same risks our troops were facing to support it. I was definitely not going out of a sense of adventure or curiosity.

The enrollment process can take up to two years, but with a great deal of help from several people (thank you, Lieutenant Colonel Kris Stevens,* Major Marc St-Pierre,† Chief Warrant Officer David Cole and the whole Primary Reserve List Headquarters crew!), I got everything done in four months. I re-enrolled in the Canadian Forces on August 28, 2007. A few days later, I was sent to the basic medical officer course at CFB Borden. On September 27, the second-last day of the course, I was asked if I could deploy to Afghanistan in mid-November.

It was not until then that I informed my group, the emergency physicians of the Sudbury Regional Hospital, that I would be off the schedule for the next five months. They were quite supportive. They picked up two months of shifts for which I had already been scheduled (including two on the Thanksgiving long weekend—thank you, J.P. and Steve!), and they covered my absence for the three months I was deployed. They even gave me three weeks off after my return. Many reservists are not nearly as fortunate.

Today was my first shift back at work in the emergency department. The group had already thrown a welcome home party for me, hosted by the irrepressible Cathy Heffernan, our social convener extraordinaire. This featured a cake with sand-coloured icing, surely a first! Despite this, there were still a lot of hugs and expressions of relief and pride on the part of my medical and nursing colleagues when I walked in. It has been a wonderful welcome back to my "normal" life.

Today was also very sad because I learned this morning that Trooper Michael Yuki Hayakaze had been killed in action yesterday. Trooper Hayakaze, a tanker with the Lord Strathcona's Horse, had been with me at FOB Leopard. He was a great kid. Quiet, calm, very competent and always cheerful and helpful.

---

* Now Colonel.

† Now Lieutenant Colonel.

Cathy and the camouflaged cake

Everyone else I served with has already left Afghanistan, so there could not have been more than two or three days left on Hayakaze's tour. He may well have been killed on his trip out of the combat area back to KAF for the flight to Canada. I can't imagine what it must be like for parents to lose their soldier son as he travelled back to them. All combat deaths are painful, but this one seems even worse.

So I close this diary in mourning for my fallen comrades and remembering why they died. There have been stark reminders recently. Since returning to Canada, I have read about two Taliban bomb attacks that occurred on February 17 and 18. The first targeted a high-ranking Afghan police officer. In Taliban eyes, the attack was no doubt successful because the officer was killed. They attacked him while he attended a public event. Over a hundred civilians died.

The second attack was aimed at a Canadian convoy. The bomb went off near one of our armoured vehicles and shook up four of our troops, only one of whom needed overnight observation before he was discharged. To achieve this negligible effect the Taliban detonated their weapon in a crowded area, killing thirty-seven Afghan civilians and severely wounding thirty more. The Taliban have not expressed any regret for either of these deliberate atrocities.

These stories were reported "in passing" in the media, with no follow-up or commentary. The reason for this was explained to me a long time ago by an American reporter I met in Africa. He told me that, when it came to deaths, one New York cop was worth:

· 2 British bobbies
· 5 French firemen
· 10 Mexican mothers
· 500 Bangladeshi typhoon victims

His cynical point was that people are rarely interested in events half a world away. That may well be true, but we are going to have to learn to care. The suffering of people anywhere in this interconnected world has an impact here in Canada, an impact that will only get worse if we do not take active measures to decrease that suffering.

This is exactly what we are doing in Afghanistan. The Taliban's disregard for fundamental human rights is total. It is precisely because we value human life far more than they do that we are waging war against them. This is something a nation must only undertake in the direst of circumstances, when one's enemies have completely crossed the line into immorality.

It is clear that the Taliban have done exactly that. Unfortunately, in conversations with many fellow Canadians since my return, I have realized that the Afghan mission usually recedes from their minds as soon as our flag-draped coffins are off the front page. All the other stories, the ones that explain and justify our participation in this war, are barely noticed.

That is tragic. If you are unsure about the mission or if you oppose it, those are precisely the stories you *should* be reading. All too often, I have discussed my time in Afghanistan with people who are "against" the war only to discover that their knowledge of the situation in Afghanistan is extremely limited.

This has to change. Our country is at *war!* Those of us in uniform are your brothers and sisters. We are dying on your behalf. Just as significantly, we are killing in your name. We are the ones who will bear the scars of these events, on our bodies and in our souls, for the rest of our lives. Canadians owe it to us to be well informed.

When they are so informed, Canadians will learn about Afghan parents who are so determined to see their children rise out of misery that they send them to school despite the very real risk that they and their children will be murdered for taking this step. Canadians will learn about the Taliban killing dozens of civilians on the chance that they might wound a single Coalition soldier. Hopefully, these Canadians will then take a moment to reflect on what life was like for the Afghans when the Taliban were in power.

And what it would be like if they returned.

So I would urge all Canadians to ask themselves two questions. The first is whether Afghan civilians are worth protecting. The second is whether the Taliban are so evil that they need to be opposed with lethal force.

The answer to the first question is self-evident. The answer to the second is self-evident as well, to me and to anyone who has spent time in Afghanistan. I hope it is clear to all who have read this diary.

This is a war we have to fight. This is an enemy we have to defeat.

Epilogue
2009

JANUARY 4 | Funeral

We buried Warrant Officer Gaétan Roberge today. Like me, he was a Franco-Ontarian. Because of his heritage, he spent his entire career in the army with the Van Doos, the Québécois infantry regiment. For the past few years, he had gotten himself posted to my reserve unit in Sudbury—the Irish Regiment of Canada, an Infantry unit—as an adviser. This enabled him to stay close to his parents and to prepare for his retirement, which he intended to spend in northern Ontario. He had planned to take that retirement when he got back from his tour in Afghanistan.

Three weeks ago, Warrant Roberge and I were at the unit Christmas dinner. He was on home leave, halfway through his tour. We spoke at length, veteran to veteran. We parted, and I wished him luck with the rest of his time in the "theatre of operations." My wishes weren't enough. A day after he returned to Afghanistan, Warrant Roberge, father of four and adored by his wife and parents, was killed by an IED.

A military funeral is a beautiful and horrible thing, and I think we did warrant Roberge proud with this one. The church was overflowing, and two of the warrant's oldest military friends gave speeches that were among the most moving I have ever heard. The actual interment was a textbook affair. In the bitter cold, two groups of soldiers—representatives from the Van Doos and a platoon from our unit—performed the protocols and ceremonial drills to perfection.

Beautiful and horrible. Yesterday, I went to the funeral parlour to pay my respects to Warrant Roberge's family. I was able to keep it together with his parents, but I broke down when I saw his wife. We had first met when she had come to hear me speak about my time in Afghanistan last year. Before I could say anything to her, she asked me to keep giving my presentations, to make sure that people understood why her Gaétan had died. I promised that I would.

The warrant's wife's reaction is fairly typical. Like the vast majority of families who have lost a loved one in this war, she has remained fully supportive of the mission. I have heard people say that these families have no choice but to do so—that to do otherwise would be to accept that their loved one died for nothing. This view is extraordinarily insulting to the bereaved. It presumes that grieving families are either dishonest or that they lack self-knowledge. If grieving widows and parents tell you that they agree with the mission, take it at face value. They felt that way before their loved one left, and they knew full well what price they might have to pay.

MARCH 12 | Orders

Before I left Afghanistan, the MMU commander had asked me if I would consider coming back for another tour. Coincidentally, he asked me this the same day my wife had told me that she would support me if I wanted to go back. Claude's experience had been an emotional rollercoaster, going though fear and anxiety (with some anger in there) through to acceptance and finally (when they told me I had set the record for longest time in the combat area by a physician) pride. I told the colonel I would consider it.

Last fall, the staff of Roto 7 started to discuss the possibility of my going back to do the same thing I had done on Roto 4—covering the

FOBs during the home leaves of the PAs assigned there. The formal message came today: I will be covering all four of the Canadian FOBS: FOB Lynx and FOB Leopard again ("Rocket Central"—great) and two others. I have to be at the first FOB on June 10 and will stay till September 17. There will be no surprises this time. This is a straight combat assignment.

This is likely to be the most intense period of the war so far. The Afghan elections will be taking place at the end of August. It is certain that the Taliban will do their best to disrupt this exercise in democracy, a system they despise. It is just as certain that we will do our best to push them into the deep desert. Or under it. It will likely be a bloody summer.

I went to tell Claude. She had been expecting this for months, but it was still difficult for her. And in what is the most hilarious coincidence, our dog chose that exact moment to throw up on the floor between us, just like our daughter Michelle did two years ago when I announced my intention to go war the first time.*

It was perhaps fated that I would get my orders to deploy again to Afghanistan this month. In the last ten days I have read two newspaper articles that encapsulate the differences of opinion one finds about the Afghan mission in our country. In the first, Prime Minister Stephen Harper was quoted as saying "we are not going to ever defeat the insurgency" and that "we are not going to win this war just by staying." † In my opinion, he could not be more wrong. As I wrote earlier, the *only* thing we have to do to win is exactly that: stay in Afghanistan long enough for education to defeat our enemies for us.

The second article appeared just three days later and reported on the news conference held by Mishelle Brown after the death of her husband, Warrant Officer Dennis Brown. Responding directly to the prime minister, she said: "We may not be able to beat the Taliban . . . There's

---

* The coincidence was a lot less hilarious when it turned out that he had puked because he had eaten a plastic bag that had blocked his stomach, which required very expensive doggie surgery.

† *Globe and Mail*, March 2, 2009, p. A11.

lots of things in our life we can't beat. But do you give up? Do you stop? Absolutely not."*

Mrs. Brown, please accept my deepest sympathies for your loss. And please accept my deepest appreciation for having put so clearly and succinctly what those of us who have served in Afghanistan feel. Nothing demonstrates this better than the inscription at the bottom of the memorial we erected in memory of Master Corporal Duchesne and Master Warrant Officer Mercier (see the February 8 entry). The photo below shows a close-up of a painting of the memorial, created by Silvia Pecota, an artist who has visited Afghanistan many times and spent longer at FOBs than any civilian I can think of. The inscription shows up much better than in my photograph.

Globe and Mail, March 5, 2009, front page and p. A12.

Nous Resterons—We Will Remain

I stated above that the only thing we have to do to win is to stay in Afghanistan long enough for education to defeat our enemies for us. Although this may not be obvious to many Canadians, it is very clear to the Taliban. They intuitively understand that an educated population will reject them, so they do everything they can to undermine the school system. I described in a footnote to the December 19 entry the destruction of schools and the murders of teachers and students by the Taliban. Last November, they took things to a new level, throwing acid in the faces of young girls on their way to school in Kandahar City, blinding one and mutilating others. A world bored by Taliban atrocities nonetheless took notice of that. Just Google "Kandahar acid."

That attack brought two things into clear focus for me. First, I am absolutely doing the right thing by going back to help fight the men who would do such things. When my daughter is able to read about the men who would maim and kill little girls for the crime of learning to read and write, I want to be able to tell her that her father stood up and did what he could to stop them. And if, after a decade of involvement and a few hundred Canadian deaths, all we can say is that the girls and boys in our area of operations got to go to school, that will be enough. Tyrannies can't survive education. A big part of me is eager to take the Taliban on again to help that to happen.

This is not to say that I am going off to war with feral glee. This next mission has me far more apprehensive than the last. I am spending a lot of time quietly looking. Looking at my limbs, hoping I don't lose any. Looking at my daughter, hoping she does not lose me.

The second thing that is clear is that we have the best allies possible in this war. Not the Americans, though their added soldiers will certainly be welcome, but the Afghans themselves. Today's *Globe and Mail* ran an article* about the school whose students suffered the acid attack. Although some of the students stayed away from school initially, nearly all of them have returned, and the school's total enrolment has nearly

---

* *Globe and Mail*, March 26, 2009, p. A14.

doubled. The same thing is happening all across the country, despite Taliban threats.

Canadians need to be more aware of this. What do we see instead, far too often? Look at the bottom of any CBC.ca story about one of our fallen. The CBC website invites people to comment, and they do in the hundreds when one of us is killed. Some are expressions of support and some express honest disagreement with the mission, but many have the point of view that "these people" are all savages and that they should be left to their own devices, that they are not deserving of our soldiers' lives, that they are "too different" for us to ever be able to understand them.

What is hard to understand about parents wanting their children to better themselves? What could be more human? These people are different from us? Yeah, right.

On the contrary, these people are just like you and me. That makes them worth fighting for.

And though I hope more than anything that it won't apply to me, I think they are also worth dying for.

MAY 31 | Departure

Going to war. A second time. What would you feel on that day?

Departure

The Fallen

These Canadian soldiers, who were killed in action, are mentioned in the diary.

CORPORAL GLEN ARNOLD
KIA September 18, 2006, Medic

MASTER CORPORAL NICHOLAS BEAUCHAMP

KIA November 17, 2007, Medic

WARRANT OFFICER DENNIS BROWN

KIA March 3, 2009, Infantry

PRIVATE DAVID BYERS

KIA September 18, 2006, Infantry

CORPORAL JONATHAN DION

KIA December 30, 2007, Artillery

MASTER CORPORAL CHRISTIAN DUCHESNE

KIA August 22, 2007, Medic

CORPORAL ANDREW "BOOMER" EYKELENBOOM

KIA August 11, 2006, Medic

CAPTAIN NICHOLA GODDARD

KIA May 17, 2006, Artillery

CORPORAL ÉTIENNE GONTHIER

KIA January 23, 2008, Engineer

TROOPER MICHAEL YUKI HAYAKAZE

KIA March 2, 2008, Armour

CORPORAL NATHAN HORNBURG

KIA September 24, 2007, Armour

PRIVATE MICHEL LÉVESQUE

KIA November 17, 2007, Infantry

CORPORAL ÉRIC LABBÉ

KIA January 6, 2008, Infantry

PRIVATE SIMON LONGTIN

KIA August 19, 2007, Infantry

WARRANT OFFICER HANI MASSOUH

KIA January 6, 2008, Infantry

MASTER WARRANT OFFICER MARIO MERCIER

KIA August 22, 2007, Infantry

TROOPER RICHARD RENAUD

KIA January 15, 2008, Armour

WARRANT OFFICER GAÉTAN ROBERGE

KIA December 27, 2008, Infantry

CORPORAL MICHAEL STARKER

KIA May 6, 2008, Medic

PRIVATE COLIN WILMOT
KIA July 6, 2008, Modio

FOR THE FALLEN

They shall grow not old, as we that are left grow old.
Age shall not weary them, nor the years condemn.
At the going down of the sun and in the morning
We will remember them.

— LAURENCE BINYON

At the going down of the sun

COURTESY MCpl KEN FENNER

We will remember them

ARTWORK BY SILVIA PECOTA